THE RANDOM THOUGHTS
Of a Philosophy Major Drop-out

The Philosophy of My Life

JAMAI WRAY

Copyright © 2019 Jamai Wray

M WRAY PUBLISHING GROUP
Jamaica, NY 11433

ISBN: 978-0-578-62696-3

Printed in the United States of America

First print 2013

Foreword

Finally, it's here! It only took him thirty-two years to write it. I've known Jamai all my life and he's been known to be jumping all over the place, not able to complete projects. But his drive and ambition have always been a big part of what motivates him, as well as myself and others to want more. Motivates you to want to do what makes you happy. Watching him defeat regret and keep pushing no matter what, teaches you to appreciate the process, and to not focus on the finish line. To never give up. He always tells me that every human has the ability to be the greatest version of themselves, it's just fear that holds them back. That everybody has something they are good at without effort, and he epitomizes that.

When he asked me to write his foreword, my question was, "Are you putting this book out seriously, or, are you having one of those moments?" He chuckled and did not reply. He just stared at me with that verbal assault attack face and said, "Are you going to do it or what?"

So, I took a self-printed copy to read, and after a few days, all I can say is, what's next? I want more. From top to bottom, it's a great read. Each piece flows fluently into the other like it's one big story. This book of random thoughts is cleverly odd. I think he may have created another genre. It has an unorthodox flow, but this is Jamai—everything about him is unorthodox.

Videl Wray

I'm thankful to all those who said no, because of them, I did it myself.

—*Albert Einstein*

Contents

Chance favors a connected mind.

—Steven Johnson

First Thought

I initially wanted to name this internal monologue *Inside My Head*, until it struck me: who am I to care about what's inside my head? I do not have a degree of higher education from any institution, so labeling myself a philosopher may not be taken seriously, respected, or considered legit. For many, labeling myself a *philosopher* means that I would have to be, or have been a student under the tutelage of some well-renowned professor from a prestigious school, or, have received some type of award recognizing achievements in this field. But being that I am not a student, graduate, or anything of the sort, and you have not yet fully decided whether you are going to continue reading to find out who I am, what I know, and want to get across in this book. You will most likely judge me as a fellow who fain would pass as a philosopher. And that's cool.

My main objective in conceptualizing this book was to philosophize my life through essays and poems, while speaking more meticulously about myself, my philosophy, and how I understand that philosophy. But somewhere along the path of creating this book, I realized I had more to offer than just pieces of my life. So adding parables, rhetoric, short stories, and comedy sketches, momentously satisfied my lingering need to fill a lifelong emptiness as it broadened the book and highlighted my versatility as a writer.

There's a span of thirteen years of material in this book. Some I am not too thrilled about, but its very existence is testimony to my growth and progression. I have always considered myself more of a moral philosopher, for my mind has always been drawn to matters of psychology: that of human behavior.

I always knew that the answer to a problem, or a more vivid understanding of it, could be found if I searched for its root inside of myself in the form of habits, as opposed to outside. I hope you acquire from this journey inside of me not just knowledge and information, or a good laugh from a short story, but a sense, however faint, of my inner struggle to fulfill my passion.

Many years after dropping out of college to follow what I now regard as false hopes. I came to realize that I had gained more than I assumed I had lost. Understanding has been my greatest achievement thus far. But knowing that I have the talent to create with words is not enough. I feel the responsibility to share what I have gained throughout my life from introspection, observation and mostly my experience.

I am just a man looking for his way through words and am grateful for your attention throughout this journey. As you read, keep in mind that some dreams stay dreams, but when keep pushing to make those dreams a reality, along the way you will find your purpose.

Philosophy

The word *philosophy* means the love of knowledge and wisdom—or the attempt to acquire knowledge. In Descartes's words, "philosophy affords the means of discoursing with an appearance of truth on all matters and commands the admiration of the simpler." Philosophizing is simply offering an explanation of one's understanding of a given fact or event based on one's own beliefs and experiences, which means anyone can be a philosopher or philosophize.

Moral philosophy is the most famous of all, for the search for knowledge and truth about the nature of man and his behaviors and beliefs is at the forefront of many past and present discourses. I believe, that a lot of what needed to be discussed and evaluated about the dealings of nature and man has already been done to an extent, making a lot of what we read now from philosophers just regurgitated thoughts. Historically, philosophers are known to have asked questions that even they could not answer because one of the elements of philosophizing is not to produce an answer, but to obtain a more vivid understanding of the topic discussed. It is about asking the right questions rather than providing an explanation, so long as there is a real pursuit for a more definitive answer to a particular question or situation, and one that goes beyond our superficial perception of it.

A philosopher is a truth seeker, a thinker, one who reflects and lives a life of reason. He is a bit more curious and meticulous than the average person and cares more about where the apple came from, than the apple itself. He is an individual who is known to be cool, calm, and collected under pressure. No matter the circumstance, he always has a great deal of equanimity.

So, can he be called nonchalant for not showing any emotion? For many years I believed people when they told me I was nonchalant and emotionless and that I did things from my head and not my heart. They were right, but it's more innate than deliberate. You unconsciously gravitate toward what interests the heart or mind, whether you understand why or not. I always knew there was a reason, so I searched until I found what I believed came close to an explanation. And what I found were traits of a philosopher, for where reason is found, understanding is obtained.

Philosophy, in the context of this book, will mainly center on the lessons and character building obtained from my experiences through my understanding of them. There are many ways and use of philosophy, but I want to focus on the love and pursuit of knowledge and the understanding thyself. An investigation into the nature of I am and into my life and principles. In this book, I give to you, the philosophy of my life.

I'm an Addict

November 26, 2006
Age: 25

My name is Jamai Wray, and I'm an addict. My addiction is to 'knowledge and understanding.' I'm addicted to books of substance. The profound essence of life as opposed to the shallow repetitious plots of urban novels. This addiction isolates me from family and friends for I'm the only one with this problem. I can be very annoying at times, why? Because I'm always correcting grammar, suggesting things to read and telling peers the word they just used doesn't exist. No, *conversate is not a word, it's converse*. I'm always preaching morality when honestly, I'm just a man of theory and little practice at this point.

Some people are comfortable with who they are and what they know. So, who am I to try to knock them out their comfort zone? I am completely unaware of how tactless I am among my family and friends. This addiction causes me to be judged by my peers. They think I think, I'm better than them. I mean no harm, but sadly, perception is reality. I've concluded in my many years of getting high that the more you know, the clearer you see, and the clearer you see, the more pain you achieve. Yes, having knowledge and understanding and being highly intellectual hurts. Especially when everybody around you is sober.

Just the other day I was asked unwillingly to step out to the recreation area in my cell because a new inmate was coming in. But I couldn't open the door. It was jammed stuck with tissue wrappings.

I was then cuffed and asked to step, excuse me, *told* to step out the cell. Two correction officers went in to open the door and had success on the first try. One of the officers said, "Next time don't stuff all that tissue in the door, or you'll be paying for it buddy." Being high and not understanding I have no wins I say, "it's mathematically impossible I stuffed that door."

"Mathematically impossible... who the sky God you think you are boy? We have a freaking Einstein over here fellows!" shouted the officer. "Please, can I expound?" "Expound? No, you can't expound. Mathematically impossible... trying to sound intelligent. You can't be that damn smart though, you're in here, aren't you. Get back in your cell. Them damn city boys." He has a point. I just shook my head and walked back into my cell. The inmates above me and next door to me joked amid themselves about my choice of words.

You see what drugs do to you? You see what my addiction does for me? How is it mathematically impossible, simple? I've been in this cell for six days now. There was anywhere from eight to ten tissue wrappings jammed into the door and I'm still on my first roll of toilet tissue, thus, making it mathematically impossible. With everyone's reaction you would have sworn I solved the mysteries of the Universe. See what happens when you do drugs and everybody around you is sober. You stick out like a sore thumb. Which is how I concluded that, I'm not wrong because I'm wrong, I'm wrong because I'm outnumbered by ignorance. I guess if I'm going to continue to get high, I might as well be around people that get high too.

The 5 W's of You

December 8, 2007
Age: 27

Looking into the mirror, I ask myself, "Who are you?"

"I am Jamai Wray."
"I didn't ask you your name. I asked, who are you?"
"I am a child of God."
"I didn't ask you for your indoctrinated origin which is influenced by your religious beliefs. Who are you?"
"I am a cocky, intelligent, wise, humble when I need to be, driven, focus and ambitious individual."
"I didn't ask you for a list of your personal character traits that makes you sound like an opportunist and clearly backed by your ego. I want to know, who are you?"

Looking into the mirror, I ask myself, "Who are you?"

"I guess I'm the sum of knowledge and experiences that I have accumulated up to this very moment in my life. Because I can say that I am this or that, and that I will do this or do that. But when a situation arises, when the test of who I am is tested, the person I think I am may not react, or act, the way I think I would."
"So, who are you?"
"I don't know."

Looking into the mirror, I ask myself, "Why are you?"

"Well, I can say that I know what my destiny is based on how I feel, what I know, the passion I have in my ability to write, and what drives me to be successful under what I define success to be. To be remembered for something great and noble and not foul and destructive. To leave behind a legacy, a body of work that reflects everything I feel I can do as a writer, which makes me believe therefore I am. But until I leave this earth and someone collectively sums up what I been through, both failures and successes, what I have done with what I know and have, or didn't do, will be the only time that the question 'Why are you?' can be answered."

"So, why are you?"

"I guess one day you'll find out because it may not be what I want it to be."
"Do you doubt yourself?"
"No, but there may be a twist of fate along the path that will ultimately be of my doing, or not. When you do find out, please put it into a book so those who walk behind me will know and understand what will then be, why I am."

Looking into the mirror, I ask myself, "When you are?"

"I seem to be more comfortable around family and friends and people that have the same drive and ambition as I have. People that read and share the same hunger for knowledge as I do. I know I am very uncomfortable around people who don't quite understand me. I don't like authority because people abuse it, or maybe I just don't quite understand myself. I guess I'm me when I'm alone. But based on my inability to give you the answer you are looking for, I don't know when I am. And if I don't know who I am or why I am, then I will be just wasting my time trying to figure out when I am."

Looking into the mirror, I ask myself, "Where are you?"

"Earth."
"No, where-are-you?"

"I guess I'm me everywhere that I go. There are many pieces and parts of my personality, so it does not matter where I am, I'm me wherever I go. Isn't that the same question as when are you?"

Looking into the mirror, I ask myself, "What are you?"

"If it doesn't serve any relevance in who I think I am, striving for what I feel I need to be, to be content with myself, does it matter? Will knowing what I am affect where I want to be? Should I really care? If I'm comfortable and content with what I know, then, once again, should it matter? See, there are too many questions, too many answers, too many religions, too many opinions, too many contradictions, and not enough facts.

Honestly, there are too many facts with too many interpretations from too many sources. Some make sense, and some cancel each other out. There are too many theories that in my travels for knowledge and understanding, are good for conversational purposes only. But at the end of the day, I have to adopt and apply some type of science of some type of knowledge to my life, giving me some type of understanding of what I think I am, so I can have a better idea of what it is I think I know, so I won't be in the limbo of my own identity. Right?"

"So, what are you?"
"Honestly, I'm content with what I think I am."
"And what is that?"

Looking into the mirror I ask myself ...

M.O.N.S.T.E.R.

(**M**any **O**f **N**one **S**eem **T**hreatened **E**veryday by **R**eality)
November 7, 2011
Age: 31

Back to the reality from the depths of my subconscious, where I'm known as a proverbial monster, maxim, and lyrical mantra. Where I'm looked upon as a God of alien origin, for I am a man of what our ancestors intended; we live from what they started as descendants of minds respectively smarter. And even though the world's oldest monuments project that we as a people have lost understanding. It would be the height of our own arrogance not to acknowledge—somewhere in between the threads of time we were taught how to live and survive from a higher consciousness. This is not the topic or target but a metaphor that **M**any **O**f **N**one **S**eem **T**hreatened **E**veryday by their **R**eality. They conveniently live in a alternate world of pretentious attributes, but I see you.

Many **O**f **N**one **S**eem **T**hreatened **E**veryday by their **R**eality but what lives inside your head are the ghosts of your darkest pasts and secrets, ghouls and goblins of your deepest fears, zombies of your failures, giants of your pride and ego, midgets of your esteem, vampires who feed on your hopes, dreams, and desires, who don't live and deny it, and don't live in denial. But yet you walk around disguised— incognito as a human hiding inside your pride. At a job that doesn't represent what you truly can provide, you hide, not quite understanding that life is what you made it. So, no matter how deep inside that cave of content you hide, pretending that you're not **M**any **O**f **N**one who **S**eem **T**hreatened **E**veryday by their **R**eality, sheltered by your own fear and apprehension, you still have to look in the mirror.

And when you look in the mirror, the M.O.N.S.T.E.R. sees you, the real you, the truth. You're just a beard on a face that needs some shaving, hitting the same bumps in life from that same old razor—the craving of your esteem to be taller is shadowed by the giants of your pride and ego, who in their own arrogance have you walking around in pretentious steps of unattainable feats—chasing a person you don't have the talent to be. To tell a lie means you're trying to be or to depict something you're not, to get me to like the person you're pretending to be.

It's nothing to lie to me, but to lie to yourself only makes you **M**any **O**f **N**one who **S**eem **T**hreatened **E**veryday by their **R**eality. When the reality of the world you live in is a nightmare surrounded by the zombies of your failures, a reality not needed to be—to succeed you need not to be reminded but reminded of how great you can be—but there comes a time when you realize that you don't have what necessitates the great one you pretend to achieve. When the zombies of your failures get the best of the giants of your pride and you slowly die in the hands of the inevitable for which you created, yes I said it, the inevitable you created, as you ascend with the ghost, ghouls, and goblins into a reality you fought so hard to escape.

And no longer are you **M**any **O**f **N**one who **S**eemed **T**hreatened **E**veryday by their **R**eality, but the reality of many whose reality eventually caught up with them no matter how fast and far they ran. So don't waste time chasing fabric too expensive to weave or a God with not enough facts to believe, well, not really, just a misconstrued interpretation of what our ancestors seen, and also don't fall victim to the monsters **I-T-H-E-R** first letter **E**. Perception is reality we all believe. I'm just saying,

RANDOM THOUGHTS

the goblins' rejections might be more realistic than the projections the giants got you so hyped up to believe, for their reality lives in magazines and on TV screens—a reflection of your bewildered societal-inflicted insecurities, I call, The M.O.N.S.T.E.R.S.

A Random Moment of Clarity

October 10, 2011
Age: 30

Majority of things we believe to be truth and fact were usually someone else's opinion conceived from their tainted unrighteous indoctrinated mind. Their opinions become our facts because they relate closely to our beliefs. Beliefs we've adopted and through repetition formed the habits of our thinking. This cycle of false teachings continues with those who have not been awarded the chance to be subjected to anything but what has been subjected to us, and these false teachings become what they now believe. Your beliefs could be based on your past experiences as well as what you have seen happen to others or on a false and misconstrued conceptualization of life and love, usually dictated to us by the voices of our environment or ignorance of others. (PARENTS)

If all your life you were told that a God exist, and that you must fear and praise this God in the sky if you want to make it into heaven and avoid hell. And I believe that God only knows itself as a thing, and that one of the main problems with humans is that we humanize God. Who am I to force what I believe onto you? But if I asked whether you can prove that your view of God is truth in compared to what I believe, and you can't, then your belief is substantiated by what I said in the first paragraph. What you believe in is a fact to you, even though I view it as an indoctrinated false teaching from a tainted mind of the society slave. Who is right, and who is wrong? Don't pay too much attention to my words and personalize them or try to find where I'm potentially assassinating your beliefs. Rather, pay attention to the message so you won't miss my point.

You can easily let dissension, aroused by insecurities and arrogance falsely infuse an argument and cause you to be distracted from what I'm saying by trying to prove your beliefs. I'm not questioning your beliefs. This discussion is not to deprecate them or you, but to uplift and open your mind. Everyone is different, and no one is better than the other. No man's belief is higher and holier than the next man. It takes a great deal of understanding to adopt this concept and be open.

You must throw yourself out there; that's the only way to know. Let life be the decoder of the things you know, the people you need, and the path you need to be on. Stand firm in your beliefs, but always be open to the possibilities of the contrary. It's what we don't necessarily believe in or know that we need to learn more about. This is where the seed of understanding is planted.

We all live off some type of reaction to others' actions, the reaction behind the action of what he or she said or, what he or she did. We are all emotional. This is why you have to focus more on humility. It's coming to terms with being content with the contrast amongst us as humans, that allows your understandings to give those who feel their truth is the truth by lowering your intellect to appease them. This is what separates the fool from the genius. The humble from the arrogant. Fom the many who don't have a clue, the many that are still soul searching. Using your emotional intelligence to degrade yourself in the moment is true power and control in the future.

Dedicate yourself to finding the authentic you. Observe what drives you to others, others to you, smile to face, joy from pain, and success from failures and discover you. Remove yourself from the bottom of thinkers into the sky of possibilities and endless knowledge.

And remember, you can have all the knowledge, formulas, sciences and philsophies, but if you don't have knowledge of self, or your fellow man, you won't be able to accurately apply what you know to a future of promise. You will just be an empty cave of profound thoughts echoing in and out of the minds of those who stroke your intellectual ego with their lack of knowledge and understanding. Once again, stand firm and believe in something. You may attract envy on your quest because of what you know. You may even outgrow close friends and start to isolate yourself. So what? It's probably what you need. Staying true to yourself and remaining open will only serve as a gravitational pull for what you need to gain and accomplish in this lifetime. It only makes the force field of the inevitable you that much stronger.

Remember, we contract not only the manners of those we keep in company but even their ways of thinking. You become, if you are not already, the company your mind keeps. You change the way you think by changing the air you breathe, the things you see, and the food you eat. Be you, do you, and accept you, and those who will surround you - will surround you with you.

And remember one thing, the Universe will not let you struggle your entire life if you are being true to yourself. You will be rewarded for this honesty. Just keep pushing your truth. For you manifest what you feel, not what you think.

Imagine That

December 28, 2008
Age: 27

A man with no imagination is a man with no vision.
A man with no vision is a man who can't see past the
length of his arm.

A man who can't see past the length of his arm is a man
who is blinded by his own ignorance.
A man who is blinded by his own ignorance is a man out
of touch with life.

A man who is out of touch with life is a man who doesn't fully
understand his reality.
A man who doesn't understand his reality blames.
A man who blames is a man who is insecure about his own
shortcomings.

A man who is insecure is a man who feels inferior among others
of intelligence.
A man who feels inferior surrounds himself with fools of like
or lesser minds.

A man who surrounds himself with fools has a false sense of
superiority and intelligence and thinks he is wise.

A man who thinks he is wise and is not will show in his
actions. And what shows in your actions reflects who you
are. So, who are you?

We're not going there again. You are whomever you
imagine yourself to be.

Now imagine that.

Mr. Napkin

Waking up in cold sweats has become the norm for me. Nightmares of floating to my death as I blow around the cold concrete of New York City haunts me, as I hope to avoid getting caught in a puddle. I stare into the mirror at the coffee stain tattooed on my crinkled face, listening to the wind hit my window, wondering if I will ever get the opportunity to catch the tears of someone in need and be more than a barstool to a drink. A muzzled sound of a phone ringing catches Mr. Napkin's ear as he searches for the sound outside his bathroom door. He floats over to the sound seemingly coming from underneath his pillow. Mr. Bounty reads on the screen as he answers.

"Hey Boss," says Mr. Napkin.
"Good morning, I may need you to come in today to cover a happy hour shift."
"I don't work happy hours you couldn't call Scott?"
"If he was available, I wouldn't be on the phone with you now would I?"
"The last happy hour shift I worked I almost didn't make it home; you know how it gets."
"It would just be a few tables until it calms down. I might be short on layers today and will need the extra cloth-power. If I see it getting out of hand, I'll pull you." Mr. Napkin sighs knowing there's no way out of this.
"Just come in to be safe," says Mr. Bounty.
"Okay, I'll be there."

Peter goes to work looking for inspiration.

"You're in earlier than expected," says Manny, Peter's boss.
"Just here to take advantage of my employee discount."
"Don't drink too much I may need you to cover a shift for me."

"Then I promise to drink as much as humanly possible on purpose and go stand outside with a huge endorsed by me sign in my hand."

"Whatever Peter," as they both laugh.

"May I get you anything sir?" asks Kelly, the barkeep.

"Yes, how about some inspiration?"

"I don't think being at a bar is the solution you're looking for."

"I've read somewhere that the same creative response your brain has to getting tired at night is the same as when you drink alcohol," says Peter.

Kelly looks both surprised and confused. "That's interesting, I guess."

"Interesting indeed. Can I get a double of 1738 neat please?"

"Coming up." Peter mumbles words under his breath while the barkeep makes his drink.

"Is that something you're working on?" asks Kelly.

"Yes, I'm entering this contest and the deadline to submit my work is the 15th of December and I don't like what I have so far. It's about me, well, a napkin actually."

"Sounds like you may be over-thinking it a bit. Trust what you have. The worst that can happen is never as bad as not participating in it at all."

"Good point," says Peter.

"Well, here's your drink, a napkin and a pencil, sign here and that will be all."

"You got it. You have such an amazing smile. If I start hitting on you in an hour or so you know..."

"I know, I know, it would be the alcohol talking."

"No, it would be me talking. The alcohol is just the little red guy on my left shoulder who controls the you-know-what in my life."

"Oh, I see. Okay, I'll remember that." Creep, she mumbles.

OF A PHILOSOPHY MAJOR DROPOUT

Peter lifts his glass and investigates the mirror, cheers. And in one motion ingurgitates his drink placing the glass firmly back down onto the counter.

"Keep it coming!" shouts Peter. Kelly places another drink onto the counter in front of him. He engorges this one just as expeditiously as the former.

"Hit me with the last double!"

"You're kidding right?" Kelly asks.

"I'm trying to cross paths when both the exhaustion and alcohol inhibits the frontal cortex at the same time, to create the equilibrium needed to reproduce twice the effect of my creative response."

"Sounds like you're almost there. You already sound smarter." Kelly says sarcastically as she walks away chuckling. Peter grabs the pencil and jots down a thought on the napkin as a neighbor chimes in.

"Excuse me, hi, excuse me Sir, my name is Cedar Woods. Can I offer you some inspiration please? Inspiration through poem?" An increasingly drunken Peter responds, "Sure."

"Like a pencil, I started out in a box with others, like in the womb of my mother, being the only creator out of millions to make it to the hand, making me special, like the first time I wrote, I took my first breath. As the years pass, the more I write the shorter my pencil, the shorter my life, the closer to death and the wiser I got. But occasionally, I have to sharpen my knowledge when my pencil becomes dull. And even when I try to erase what I wrote from the paper, if you pay close attention you can still see the words, covered up by words, to cover up my past of verbs that always seem to come back to the paper, as if what I'm writing and wrote was already written. Making the way I live my life – the way I look at life – and the way I hide from life through words, something like a pencil."

"That was awesome!"

RANDOM THOUGHTS

"Thank you. It's just that every time I perform it there's always some jerk in the audience that says, 'but you are a pencil,' like I don't know I'm a pencil. Which is my only issue when performing in holes-in-the-wall, but I take what I can get you know?"

"Definitely. I don't care what you are that was great. I can come up with something creative like that, but I could never finish it."

"Do you have any pieces completed?" asks Cedar.

"Heck yeah."

"Then what are you waiting for, you need to go out and perform them. You will never know how great you are until you stop procrastinating and challenge yourself."

"He procrastinates because deep down he knows he's chasing a person he doesn't have the talent to be."

"And who are you?" asks Peter.

"My name is J.W Napkin, a one-time aspiring writer." And where did he come from covers Cedar Woods face as he says,

"You sound like you created excuses and confused your lack of focus and dedication with not having what it takes."

"Negative. I just decided to deal with reality, and at some point, you will have to deal with it too. You'll realize when it's too late that all this time you spent writing was just a hobby," says Mr. Napkin facing Peter.

"Don't listen to him Peter. If you don't fight for what you believe in consistently, then you'll end up just like this thin layer of protection over here, a.k.a, J. W. Tissue." Mr. Napkin gestures in disagreement and says, "When you have kids and a wife to support it's called being a responsible adult. Yes, I hate the fact that I'm subjected to these places for employment because of the texture of my fabric. There was a time I wasn't content with the description that comes with why I was manufactured, but how many no's are enough?" asks Mr. Napkin.

"I can understand where you're coming from because the more rejections I get, the more I feel distant from what initially drove my passion to write," says Peter.
Nodding his head and giving a reassuring smile Mr. Napkin says,
"That's because you're slowly beginning to come into the dark side my son."
"Don't encourage him. Peter, look, there's going to be days you want to give up and days you feel at your best. Just make the needed adjustments and master your craft. Don't interpret the constructive criticism you receive into you don't have what it takes. You don't want to be a bitter old man questioning whether you dedicated yourself enough." Unresponsively, Peter stares rubbing his eyes. The drinks are in full control as he chuckles mumbling, Cedar Woods and Mr. J.W Napkin.

"Kelly, one more drink please and that's it. I feel it coming. I feel my creative juices boiling."
"Bar is closed. Sorry."
Before he can respond, Peter passes out onto the counter.

"Ouch!" says Kelly as his head hits the wood. Thirty minutes passes by and Manny comes over and taps Peter on his shoulder.
"Peter, Peter get up!"
"Yeah, yes, I'm up. What happened?"
"We're closing. Are you okay dude?"
"I'm okay. Why?"
"Because you were talking to yourself the entire night."
"I was?"
"Yes" says Mr. Bounty.
"Did I work? Did you need me?"
"No, but thanks for coming in, I appreciate it."
"No problem." Peter grabs the napkin and pencil off of the counter, places them inside his pocket and heads towards the exit scratching his head. *Mr. Napkin...hmm.*

The 5-Story Building

5th floor
We have a better view.

4th floor
Yeah, and it's quiet up here too.

2nd floor
Well, if there was a fire, it would be safer to jump from here.

5th floor
That's silly. Who jumps from the 1st floor?

2nd floor
You never know. And it's the 2nd fl.

1st floor
Plus, we're more accessible.

Even though the 3rd floor was in the middle, he never got in between, until one Sunday he was asked his opinion.

5th floor
I know you hear us every day, what do you think?

3rd floor
I think all four of you are crazy.

1st floor
Why would you say such a thing?

3rd floor
Because it doesn't matter who has the better view, who is more accessible or where it's safer to jump, we are all in the same building.

On the J

Journal Entry
October 17, 2012
Age: 31

My head wobbles from side to side as it rests on the window of the J train on my way to my girlfriend's house. The image of my cell phone rattling against my desk plays in my mind as I clutch my backpack. My backpack — or my survival kit, as I call it — it houses my work uniform, toothbrush, soap, deodorant, undergarments, and other cosmetic-related items. It's only been a couple of days since the news, but I can already see that this is going to take some endurance. Nothing I am not used to. Just at this particular age and stage in my life, I just wonder.

The image of me breaking away from my keyboard to reach over and grab my phone plays in slow-motion in my head as I swipe my pass code. I notice a message from my landlord that reads, "I'm sorry for the short notice, but you have until Monday to remove all of your belongings from the apartment. I'm so sorry, but you have to move out." In just a matter of seconds, I'm finding out that I have six days to find somewhere to stay. I didn't know what to think. I knew this wasn't a joke but in awe of how random it was. Here I am at my computer, putting the finishing touches on this book, and in just seconds, I'm told I won't have a place to live in six days.

The first person I called was my brother to secure the transportation of my belongings. Then I called my mother to make sure I had a place to put my belongings. Then I called my girlfriend, who in my defense couldn't believe that at a time like this, with my trying to finish this book and move on professionally in my life, this would have happened. Clueless on my next move, she offered me room if I wanted to stay with her, but at this point I don't know what I'm exactly going to do as far as living arrangements. I just want to get my things out of here safely.

I just sat at my computer speechless. This can't be real, I said to myself, but it was. I went to the LQ store, which was conveniently across the street from my building, to help shelter this pain. I'm on my own doing everything right, finally making progress both personally and professionally, and boom, in six days I will be homeless.

I can see the look on my mother's face now. This is embarrassing. I really hate needing people, but I don't know what to do, and she's the only one that can help me. I just can't see myself back under her roof. We don't mix well at all. I'd rather roam the streets, I told myself as I ask God, "What do you want from me? What have I done now? I thought I paid my dues to society. Why is this happening? What do you want from me?"

"Next stop Gates Avenue," the train conductor says over the loudspeaker. I get up, and put my backpack on my back, and rest my head on the train door, hurt and sad.
"I just want to do what I know you gave me the gift to do; that's all, God. What do you want from me?"

Miserable

August 24, 2000
Age: 19

Being miserable, to the point where I'm getting headaches from thinking too much and too hard. So many things to do in a short period of time. Tuition is due, but how do I pay it when I don't have a dime. When I have nobody to help me. When I feel so alone. I'm only nineteen years old. Am I supposed to be this miserable?

At one point, life couldn't be better. Everything was going my way. I'm in college. I'm working. I mean, what more can I ask for? That's when the clouds started to form. When the what goes up must come down theory took effect. Getting fired from my job was the beginning. Having more time on my hands was the setup. Instead of looking for another job, I take a vacation, and that unoccupied time became occupied with females.

Being a young man of nineteen years, I'm not turning anything down. I have standards, of course, but this lifestyle is still so new to me. Knowing it's time to focus on working and going to school and that girls aren't going anywhere is easier said than done. I can't help myself.

Go to school, bro. Handle your business. But how can I go to school when I can't pay the fare to get me there and back. I lost my job at a telemarketing company for finishing a survey after the caller hung up. I was at the last 5 questions and didn't see the harm. Unfortunately, my supervisor was monitoring my phone calls and fired me later that day.

32

Due dates on bills are here. What do I do? I never thought doing so well would be so hard, so the only option with no job is to lay up with my girlfriend who is doing just as bad as me. Slowly but surely going backwards. It seems like when I want to do good and do the right thing, what I'm working for takes so long to achieve, and when I'm doing bad, what I don't need comes so fast.

Being miserable, everything I hoped for, all my dreams I can see flushing down the toilet. Everything I visualized is becoming blurry. I don't want to give up, but unconsciously, I already have. My friends go somewhere to eat. The look of being broke is on my face, so someone offers me a meal. What do I do when I want to do so much? I have so many ideas, but I don't know where to start.

I know I need help; I just don't know who to ask. All I have is my mother, but I don't think she likes me enough. I don't like her either, or her husband. I'm starting to look how I feel, busted and down and out. Down on my luck and out of money. Is everybody lives around me so messed up that what I'm going through goes unnoticed? Nothing positive seems to exist anymore.

I'm living at home with my mother, paying no bills, no rent, but doing what I want when I want. My mother and her husband always get into arguments over me. The conflict between my parents is not making my situation look any better. I hear them at night arguing about me.

My stepfather doesn't understand why my mother puts up with my crap and thinks she should put me out. My mother tells me if he leaves, I have to go. I guess choosing him over me makes sense. I am becoming a man and need to stand on my own two feet. But it's so hard. I want to finish school, but I don't have any money.

I really miss my father. Daddy, why did you have to leave me? Why did God take you from me? Why am I being punished like this? Why don't you ever answer me God?

Being miserable, a feeling I do not want to feel again. I never did like hide-and-seek growing up, but when you're miserable that's the best game to play. Hiding from everybody refusing to go outside because you're scared of what you might do. As you sit in a room listening to music that plays as an assist to your feelings of depression, your L.I.F.E. is defined as Living In Fear Every day. Living in a world where you fall with the hope and strength to get back up. But I fell, and the feeling in my legs are getting weaker. Like a doctor telling me I will never walk again. Never shoot the ball again. And the saddest part is I don't have anybody telling me everything will be all right. That everything in the future is bright. That I'm going to get help, finish school and get my degree, a good job and a bad wife.

I can do this by myself, and I will. It's time to do my thing and get up off my butt and make something happen. It's time to stop parading around the house in a boat that sunk months ago. I get it in me; all right, it's time for a change. I must at least finish this semester. Oh yeah, I must find a job because my mother is about to kick me out. I'd need rent money, and I must pay my tuition soon to finish this semester. That's right, I was supposed to be in a talent show for my school and didn't go. Exams are coming. I'm running out of time to make up for other classes. Don't get caught jumping the turnstile. (I don't need that!) I hope this girl is not pregnant. So many mother loving baby fat things going on that my mind becomes over flooded and drowns as my hand stretched out from under the water and remains. This can't be life. This can't be life. Does anybody see my hand? Does anyone see me drowning?

Looking Back Thirteen Years on Being "Miserable"

I never thought writing would be the focal point of my life. I never thought that without it I would feel empty and inadequate. At that time in my life, the paper was the only person I had to talk to. That was the only way I had to express myself.

I remember feeling very alone. I was just finishing up my first semester at LaGuardia Community College full-time and was working behind the school at a telemarketing company full-time as well. I was fired because I continued to complete a survey on my own after the caller hung up. With the pressure of paying for school full-time, working full-time, and then being fired, I fell into a great depression that resulted in my dropping out.

On top of that, my mother didn't allow females in the house, so I was sneaking behind her back, getting caught, and being threatened with being kicked out.

I didn't even know I wrote the "Miserable" piece until the next morning. All I remember was getting extremely intoxicated the night before and contemplating suicide. I never told anybody about this until now. It was really rough for me. So much was going on in my life, and I guess I did a great job of concealing it. As I look back, I realize now how important support, love, and someone to talk to are in a child's life.

Young and Restless

August 14, 1999
Age: 18

Young man, why so restless?
I understand you're young, but why so reckless?
You have access to everything and still disconnected.
You're failing in school because you put no effort.
You get the benefit of the doubt because you're an
adolescent, but always remember to respect the
disrespected.

And everything you see or hear is not the truth, so don't
accept it. You don't have to sing, rap, or dance to relay a
message. I do what I do because I've been blessed with.
You don't know what to do in life, but who did at your age?

I want to do this, I want to do that,
but the "I want to's" might change. It's great to be young
but being restless will take you out the game.

So, try to eliminate the "I should haves" before it's late in the
4th of life's unpredictable game.
Some grow old and never change.
And at this moment it might just be a phase,
so don't give up and continue to play the game.
Because being young and restless turns into being old and
tired, and at that stage it's no longer a phase.
Don't wait too long to wake up, and remember,
you control this game.

Never stop moving.

Whenever you go to someone who does not want to be school on life,
he feels as if you're talking down to him. But whenever a person
who wants to be schooled on life comes to you, he appreciates it.
The contrast is this: the person who feels deprecated insecurities
becomes anger, whereas the one who appreciates
your insight, prospers.
—Jamai Wray

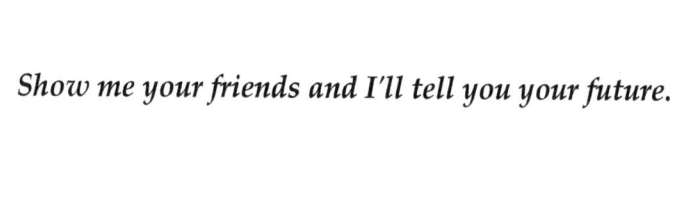

Show me your friends and I'll tell you your future.

You Were There

November 19, 2001
Age: 20

You were there when I decided to leave for out of state. You were there when we stole money from the Cooks to get to New York. You were there when the first car we took broke down on us on the highway, and we had to sit out in the cold waiting for someone to help us. You were there when we slept in the cold in a car covered with snow. You were there when we had to stay with my friend in his girl's mother's house when you couldn't stand him.

You were there when we bought our first apartment together. You were there when we had to sleep on the floor because we didn't have a bed, and it was the dead middle of winter. You were there when we got our first home entertainment system, and our neighbor underneath us complained almost every day because the music was too loud. You were there when we didn't have any money to wash our clothes or pay our bills. You were there when we had to jump out of cabs because we couldn't afford the fare.

You were there when we finally got an air bed. It got a hole that we couldn't find, and when we woke up on the floor the next morning. You were there when we wrote a check to ourselves. You were there when we didn't have any money to buy food, and when we did have food, it was just cold cuts, pasta, and Ramen soups, sometimes we ate cake mix— whatever filled our stomachs. You were there when we tried to sell the home entertainment system but forgot to take the R.A.C. sticker off. You were there when we stole that Honda from Connecticut with intentions to sell it in New York, but couldn't because we didn't have a title.

We went through four states to Virginia just to end up back in New York, in the Bronx, in Hunts Point, where we almost ended up behind bars. In that whole week, we didn't shower and barely ate. You were there when we received our first eviction. You were there watching my back when I fought my friend. You were there to call my mother when I got out of hand.

You were there when we purchased our first car. You were there when that car broke down on us on our way to Texas, and I had to push it a mile to a mechanic that we couldn't pay. Remember that old couple that paid for the work done on the car because we reminded them of themselves when they were our age? You were there. You were there when we pulled into that police station in a stolen car and made it out alive. You were there when we were driving down the I-95 with no gas money on our way to Texas from Connecticut in an '89 Ford Escort with no windshield wipers that we didn't realize weren't there until that storm in Delaware hit. Remember along the trip when you had to ask people for money so we can have some gas and something to eat just to get us to the next hour or the next gas station?

You were there when your parents took me in. You were there when we had to walk in the hot Texas sun to find a job. You were there when our car ran out of gas on the highway in Texas with no air conditioner, and we had to wait an hour for someone to realize we were stranded. You were there when our brakes on our car went, risking our meaningless life every time we drove it. You were there when we ran into the back of a Jeep because of those faulty brakes. You were there when we wanted to kill ourselves.

You were there when we got our second apartment. Remember sleeping on the floor because we threw away that air bed? You were there when we were pulled over by a cop, with no license, no registration, no insurance, in a stolen car with marijuana in it, just to be told we had to tape up a broken headlight. You were there when I was arrested, and your father had to bail me out. You were there when we had to sell a $2,000 charcoal- colored Italian leather sofa set (that wasn't bought in the first place), a TV, a kettle (birthday present), and vacuum cleaner for $400.

You were there when the car we bought for $700 had to be sold for $65. You were there when I had to go back to New York, knowing that it would be breaking our lease and your parents would have to pay for every month they didn't rent the space out. You were there when I needed comfort and a shoulder to rest my head. You were there. You were there when you asked, when is our next meal coming from; how are we gonna pay rent; how are we going to get these brakes fixed; how are we going to get money to get back to New York; where are we going to sleep; we need to get some gas; what if the cops pull us over; it's cold out here; damn, it's too hot out here; we need a car; I'll be home soon, baby; how are we going to go about this; what if we get caught; is this the end. I got fired today. We're about to be evicted. A miscarriage, another miscarriage; I hope we make it; will we ever get out of this; I can't stay here anymore; are you coming or what; I'm yours forever, I hate you; I love you; I can't take anymore, God.

No matter how hard it was and how much your parents begged you to come with them to Texas, which we eventually did. For every tear, every sad song and hungry night. Every fight, every uncertain step we made it through, I'm happy you were there. And I'm sorry. It still remains the toughest time period of my life.

Why Me?

2002, almost a year later, Jamaica, NY
Age: 21

She knocked on my door, clearly not in her right mind. By the looks of her clothes and her pacing back and forth, something was obviously bothering her. I took her out to Red Lobster in the 1982 Cadillac Seville she had driven up from Texas. I remember pulling my money out my pocket to pay for the meal and her quickly blaming herself for the financial problems we were having while living together. "I don't blame you," is what I said, being humble. At this particular time, I was doing very well for myself working as a utility worker in a milk plant in Queens.

We went back to where I was living because she wanted to stay the night. I kept saying to myself that something was just not right. She went on to explain about a babysitting job she had and how she was fired for something not in her control. It obviously bothered her because she couldn't seem to let it go. I had to work that night, so I prepared myself for a four-hour nap to get up at 7:30 pm for my 8:00 shift. When we went to bed, her exacts words were, "Don't try it." Little did she know I wasn't even contemplating it. At least fifty pounds lighter than the last time I had seen her, she looked terrible. I was worried.

Twenty minutes into my nap, she started to whisper to me that she heard voices in her head, voices telling her to sell herself for money, voices telling her she was no good and not worth it and to kill herself. I remember her telling me about those voices a couple years back but never took it seriously because she never did. She began talking to herself under her breath about what had transpired in Texas with that job she had.

She kept saying how everything was okay until that little devil girl (I assumed the little girl she was watching) lied about her.

I asked her if she was all right. She sat up and told me she had to show me something. I turned the light on as she went for her bag. I couldn't believe my eyes when I saw it: an all-black 380 handgun. I asked her if it was loaded as she sat in the chair swirling it around. My heart was on overdrive. It was clear she was unstable. I did not know her intentions, so I moved myself closer to her to kill the space.

"Don't worry; the safety is on," she said. I guess she could see the anxiety on my face. Going back to sleep was not an option at that point. She told me that she would be leaving in the morning to go back to her aunt's house. That's where she was staying, or trying to relocate, I presumed. All day at work she was on my mind. I was clueless, no thoughts on what she wanted o r why she even came to see me.

The next evening around 7:00 pm she came back over. She wanted to sleep. While she was knocked out, I watched the news. "Breaking news just in" flashed on the TV screen as the words left the female anchor's mouth. "Police are looking for a suspect in connection to a shooting." When they posted her picture and said her name, my mouth just dropped in awe. I could not believe what I was seeing. She had just shot a pharmacy worker in the chest. I was in complete and utter awe. There she was lying in my bed at that very moment, like nothing ever happened. She must have just done it and came over right after. Why would she do that to me? I was harboring a fugitive. Scared to death and unclear about what to do, I searched for the weapon. When I found it, I hid it from her in my safe. I couldn't let her go back out like that. She was liable to get herself killed. I didn't know what to do.

I couldn't tell anybody because there was no one to tell, but sooner or later, with her coming back, somebody was going to see her. All I saw in my head was the cops shooting and asking questions later. She was that unstable. Voices were telling her to sell herself and that she was no good; there was no telling how she was going to react. If I called the cops on her and turned her in, I would just be a snitch. I went through her bags to try to find a cell phone to locate her parents' number. The least I could do was contact them. Nothing. No cell, not anything. I prayed I had some contact information in my cell, but I didn't.

She awakened an hour later as I sat there bewildered. I immediately told her she was just on the news and that the police were looking for her. Her reply was, "Yeah, I know." She said she went to the pharmacy with her aunt to develop some pictures and decided to do a robbery. When she pulled the gun out on the clerk, she laughed at her because she didn't take her seriously. So, she shot her in the chest and then came over.

"Why would you come back here?"
"Where else was I going to go," she replied.

Then I decided some have looked at as foul and unfair to her. Some believe I should have sent her away instead of doing what I did. Thinking of saving my own ass and her mental health, I called the cops and turned her in the next day while she was asleep. My landlord answered the door and let the detectives in. When he found out that I had her there, he went off in a verbal rage. All I could say in my defense was, "What would you have done in my shoes? She came to me. Whether it was to make a choice for her or not, she gave me that power. I didn't know what she was up to. I was just being a friend. I didn't know."

He looked at me with complete understanding and just walked off. Once it made the paper and they labeled me her boyfriend, I knew I wouldn't hear the last of this. The streets labeled me a snitch, a sellout. Looking back at it now, maybe I could have just sent her away. Would it have helped? That's never to be known. I just did what I thought was right. For me, and for her.

She never went to jail; instead they put her in a hospital. I visited her and took her food for months until she begged me not to come up to see her anymore. She was never mad at me. Well, at least she never expressed it. After all we have been through, it's impossible not to wonder where she is and how she's doing now. I'm sorry.

Every decision you make must benefit not just you and the moment, but others as well as the future.
—Jamai Wray

RANDOM THOUGHTS

You can't serve two Gods

January 5, 2007
Age: 26

It's the summer of 2006, my back was against the wall. I threw one of the biggest parties in South Side Jamaica Queens the following summer and was expected to do a follow up, but things fell through with the venue I wanted. I just started M Wray Enterprise and was finishing up the design of my website. I needed logos and trademarks. I was putting together greeting Cards, getting my short novel published and working on a prototype for my sneaker shoe, the M Wray's. I was all over the place trying to make something happen. I typed up an 8-page business proposal and shopped my ideas around looking for an investor. First place was my job at Bartlett Milk Dairy.

My boss Kenny allowed me to have the meeting in the company's conference room. Presentation went well, but I was shot down. After the company I was working for turned me down as well as a few more small businesses I gave up. Coming home from work one day I met this man named Paul. He claimed to be a boxing promoter that works with Don King. It was early June and very hot outside when he mistook me as a boxer. I was shirtless and because of my physique that can be assumed. I told him I wasn't a boxer and that I was a recording artist. "Funny" he says, "I'm currently looking for an artist to open a boxing match for me in Aruba are you any good?" "Heck yeah." I replied. I took his number and scheduled a lunch with him later that week. I went over numerous ideas with him and what I was trying to do. He shown some interest but wanted to hear my music. I played a song I recorded named "Rise" and he went insane. "This could be, like, the anthem to boxing.

This is great," he says. I'm just smiling and happy that he's enjoying it. "This is what I need you to do, Jamai, right?" "Yes." "Put together a press package. Get some hats, some T-shirts print up as many copies of this as you can, I'm flying you to Aruba." This is exactly the big break I need. So now I have a show in Aruba where I have to get shirts, hats, CD's, oh, how can I forget; I have a daughter being born in August, a mix-tape to get pressed up that I was working on before this, a book to publish, greeting Cards to make, a prototype for my shoe and a party to put together, all this, with no money. The passion is there, but no resources.

I tried just about every possible thing. So now, after being let down by people who told me investing into me would be too risky, I started to contemplate robbery. I didn't want to, but I didn't know what else to do. I'm in my house pacing back and forth because it's down to the wire. I'm both fearful and indecisive and don't want to do anything stupid. In my heart I knew what I was contemplating was wrong. I had way too much to risk. Too many people were counting on me and this can jeopardize everything I've accomplished so far. But upstairs in my mind I was hearing something else.

My mind was telling me, you know what you have to do, make it happen. You know scared money don't make money. This is it; you do this and its smooth sailing from here. Yes, my mind and heart were on two different pages in the same book. So, I decided based on my circumstances and what I felt I needed. It was the only thing I haven't tried. Sometimes you must take a step back, to move two steps forward. By any means necessary is what I told myself. This is for my dream, for what I believe in. There's nothing wrong with doing bad things if your intentions are right. That's what Jay-Z did. Why can't I do the same?

After making my decision I started robbing truck drivers at the end of their routes. I also was robbing customers I delivered milk to because I knew where they kept their stash. But it wasn't enough. I needed at least $100,000 dollars and all I had accumulated thus far was about $3,500. So, I decided to go back to where I robbed three drivers at and stick the armor truck up that picked up money every Thursday at 10:10am. I'm at the location, heart was pounding, Spike, a colleague of my brothers noticed me and looked at me in concerned as the look in my eyes was not what he was used to seeing in me.

The armor truck didn't show up on time and I had to get out of there because I felt everybody was watching me. I noticed a driver walking to the office and I decided to at least make my coming out worth it. I pulled my gun out on him and somehow ended up dropping it. We got into a tussle and I was overpowered when a co-worker of his arrived. They held me down as the guy put the gun to my head and pulled the trigger. The gun went off. "Click", but nothing. The only reason I'm alive is because I never carried a loaded weapon. Robberies can quickly turn to a homicide. But if the gun went off and a bullet lodge into my head resulting in my death, it would have been justified. I was wrong. I had the passion to pursue my dream and was willing to do what I needed by any means necessary to achieve it. Problem is, you can't get a positive from a negative. I was locked up shortly after and sentence to 3 years in a New York State Correctional facility for possession of a firearm. I was convicted on one count of "Serving two Gods."

Afterthought

Passion is a great thing when harnessed positively. Too much of it without the right focus, patience, and understanding can close a lot of doors, burn a lot of bridges, and scar the chances of you ever living out your dream. I was young, reckless, and naive. I thought that as long as what I intended to do was to for my dreams, it didn't matter what I did to obtain it, but it doesn't work that way. Whether it happens at that moment or not, you will pay for your wrongdoing. Remember, nothing built on sand will stand. The right intentions mean nothing when your actions contradict it. You will reap what you sow. Always do the right thing, no matter how easy doing wrong may seem. Nothing worth having is easily attained. Always stay positive.

Da Bum, Da Blind Man, and Da Alcoholic

August 8, 2004
Age: 23

Coming this fall to channel 23 ET.TV is a show that will bring bums, the blind, and alcoholics together. Where panhandling on trains and New York City garbage cans is a source of survival. Where the life story of a bum will bring you to tears, the shame of an alcoholic will arouse your deepest fears, and the isolation of a blind man will have you thanking the lord you're not. Here's a preview of what Shane and Wesley calls "embarrassingly unique." "Two hands way up on creativity." "Writing at its best," raves the critics. Here's a scene from the trailer that has Emmy written all over it.

The Blind Man is walking down the street whistling as Da Bum and Da Alcoholic argue on the corner about two quarters.

Da Bum
Look a Charles over there with his blind ass. Ever since he got that new dog and stick, he's been walking around like he got two new golden eyes or something.

Da Bum chuckles.

Da Alcoholic
Yeah, right.

Da Bum
Hey, Charles. (*Watch this*) Hey, Charles. If I was to throw a pair of eyes at you, would you see them coming?

Da Bum and Alcoholic laugh. (Da Alcoholic: "Would he see it coming?")

Da Blind Man

And if I told you I just dropped two nickels and a slice of bread, would you go back and pick it up?

Da Bum

It depends. If you dropped a mayonnaise package with it then I might give it some thought, you blind motherfucker. But at least I can see what I'm eating.

Da Blind Man

But can you afford it?

Da Alcoholic

Can you see it?

Da Blind Man

Do you buy it?

Da Bum

Don't need to. All I have to do is make sure I'm at 125th street and St. Nick by 9:00am for breakfast and back by 12:30 for the lunch special garbage can buffet.

Da Alcoholic

Yup, and right now I'm about to go get me a bottle of Hennessey with money I can see myself counting.

Da Alcoholic

Hey, Red, can you take me drunk I'm home?

Da Bum and Da Alcoholic laugh hysterically.

Da Blind Man

See, that's exactly what is wrong with your kind; you see'ers. You have eyes but are still blind. You can see what's in front of you and at the same time be blind to what's in front of you.

Everything you need is in arm's reach, but your lack of sight makes it seem a galaxy away. And look what you made of your life. You had every opportunity to be more than what you are, and you still ended up losers. You'd be better off blind. At least you would've had a better excuse to be in the crap the two of you derlict's are in.

Da Alcoholic
Here you go again, always have to go deep and hit below the belt. And I have an excuse: it's a genetic condition that runs in my family, Mr. Genius. You just mad you bite your fingers when you eat a burger motherfucker.

Da Bum and Alcoholic chuckle as the Alcoholic takes another swig from his bottle.

Da Blind Man
But can you count how many fingers you have in front of you, you dumb schmuck? And what's your excuse?

Da Bum
This is a childhood dream. As a child, I was asked what I wanted to be when I grow up, and I said a bum. I'm free from the bills my parents always complained about. I have free medical. I do what I want to do when I want to do it, like my father prayed he was be able to do. I don't have the stresses of the everyday man, and I don't live to pay anybody back. I live for myself and is debt free.

Da Blind Man
So, you chose to be a bum, and from the sounds of it, you blame your parents. That has to be the dumbest thing I ever heard in my life. You have mental problems, and you need help. Does seeing a psychiatrist fit into your B.U.M. benefit plan loser?

Da Alcoholic
You ain't no better than us.

Da Bum
Hey, Red, answer me this: why is it that a blind man walks so damn slow?

Da Alcoholic
What type of question is that, it's obvious? It's because the motherfucker can't see where he's going.

Da Blind Man
No, stupid, it's because I know that where I'm going takes time.

You can learn more from a fool than a fool from you, but if you treat a fool like a fool, then the fool is you. —**Jamai Wray**

My Journey Up North: The Bus Ride

December 16, 2006
Age: 25

An anxious night led to a morning that almost seemed like it would never come. As her keys rattled against my bunk and her flashlight forced my eyes to open, the sound of my unpronounceable name quickly brought me back to reality. I'm in jail. Chained at the ankles and wrist to my waist, I step outside to breathe the city air one last time. Taking as much into my lungs as I can, I climb onto the bus to be strapped in, as I watch my freedom drive away. The trees stood up like dead corpses frozen in captivity. The watchers of the land, I called them. Each town we drove through seemed dead and deserted, like the background scenery of a winter painting. As the sky darkens, the vast land and valleys conjure visions in my head of how beautiful it would look in the summer season. Up here winter has arrived.

The streets were empty as the wind whistled by. There's something very soothing about seeing no life. It almost feels like I walk the earth alone, just me and my thoughts. There's no rushing to work or bumping into anyone trying to get to their destination, no noise or distraction, just peace. Despite the fact we are driving north, it almost feels like the South, where New York City must feel like going into the future for the people who populate this land. Wherever they are. We reached our first destination in Oneida, New York, where a drop of twenty-nine inmates was made, and lunch was served. Now take a second as you read this to visualize a small plastic bag, that contains two cookies, two quarter water drinks, and two slices of ham and cheese, with four slices of bread, each wrapped individually. Got it? Great.

Now imagine me sitting down with my hands cuffed together and chained to my waist, trying to put a sandwich together with very little mobility as I lean over. Got it? Great. Now imagine me leaning down to take a bite and one of the sandwiches and both cookies falling off my lap and onto the floor and the look on my face. Got it? Good. These are the things I must endure as punishment for a crime against the state. I must be disciplined, smart, and understand that I have no wins. So, no matter how I feel about this situation, I have to remember that it is me that put me here. Accept responsibility, learn, and move on.

We drove another two hours to Watertown, New York, where I stayed overnight. That following morning, I was transported to my final destination, Gouverneur, a very small town about thirty miles from Canada. My foot hit the hard grass as my shackled ankles barely stepped down from off the bus. The driver had one more trip to make farther up north to drop the remaining inmates off. The air is crisp. It almost feels like I stepped into another atmosphere; you can taste the difference. The setup was like an army camp or something, I guess. After leaving the infirmary from taking a X-rays and having tests done to see if I was healthy, I stepped back outside on the compound, as I put my hat on and   just looked around the wooded area and realized that I would be spending the next three years of my life confined.

Awkward Moment

I arrived in the dorm I would be staying in minutes before they called us to go to chow. Undernourished for the last few days, some hot food would have been great at that moment. So, as I unpacked, I didn't realize that that's where everybody was heading until it was too late.

The officer had no sympathy when I told him I didn't know, and that I had just arrived. It was 6:00 pm, and breakfast was not until 7:00 am. I was in transition, so with no funds available and no food, I was pretty much screwed until the morning. Then the awkward moment comes when you must decide. There is a stereotype hugely considered to be taken seriously in these conditions. From the stories you hear, taking handouts is the one thing you do not do in jail. There is always something cryptic behind it. At least, that's what you think. I wanted to say no, but my common sense wouldn't let me, although common sense out in the world is not the same for in jail. It's deeper than just the physical. It's more mental. You can and will be tried.

He must have seen what transpired because ten minutes later an inmate came up to me and offered me some food, a few Ramen noodle soups and some winter garments. It felt genuine. He seemed sincere. And because his aura said more than the perception I initially had based on the stereotype; it wasn't a problem to take it from him. It's just sad that in my environment we are so used to deceit that we don't recognize love when it's right in our face. We automatically assume the opposite, which is not always a bad thing. Defenses must always be up and alert. But you also don't want to block your blessings when an angel is standing right in front of you.

Backyard Blues

Journal Entry
October 13, 2012
Age: 31

Sitting on the back porch, I am mad that I have to wait until my sister gets up so I can get into the house. Good thing it's not that cold outside. I'll just lie down and take a nap. Let me send my sister the text first and let her know I'm still out here in the back on the patio. I'm also taking that trip out to Brooklyn later to my girl's house to go to work from there, so that's another journey. Some would suggest the smart thing to do would be to get a key from my mother. But I don't feel the need to. I don't want that safety net. I prefer the pain. I'm a soldier.

The last thing I want to do is get comfortable or even to show that I'm getting comfortable at my mother's house. That keeps the hunger there and satisfies my pride as well. It makes sense to use this time to save money and kill two birds with one stone. It's a damn shame I put myself through the things I do, but I'm here, surviving as usual, with another story to tell. I have been spending more time with my daughter and helping her mother out, so at least there is some good that's coming from this so far. Some light always seems to shine through the dark. So, for that I am blessed. This is not a good time to be weak and pessimistic, but if it's not one thing, it's another. Like I'm fighting some never-ending story of what it takes to be a loser?

I am grateful to be working though. That's a major stress reliever. If I'm making money, there's not much room for excuses. Maybe there are some mismanagement issues, but I've always maintained and lived within my means. I just can't believe I'm lying back here on the patio, waiting for my sister to awake just so I can get into wash, nap, and head back out again. Besides my being able to save money and hang out with my daughter more, it's my pride that's messing with me, knowing that I'm still struggling at this point in my life to achieve something I may not be successful at hurts.

Holding all this in and not showing the face of this inner cloud of anxiety is what makes me strong, I guess. To continue to show confidence and be optimistic and fight is the healthiest thing to do at this point. But as I lay in the backyard looking at the blue sky after a hard day of work, I'm stuck with time to think about my reality, and my reality is that up to this point in my life I haven't done nothing but dream.

The Attributes of a Man

June 26th, 2008
Age: 27 years old

It is neither the amount of money earned nor the number of degrees that determines who is or who is not a man. For an individual can have secured both and still be emotionally immature, irresponsible, and insensitive to the rights and needs of other human beings, even to the point of neglecting his own family. Work is dignity, and the individual who works for a living to secure the needs of himself and those who are dependent on him is manifesting attributes of manhood. Such a man is more valuable, responsible, and conscious of the needs of his loved ones.

According to the dictionary, the word, "man" comes from the Latin or Greek word "Homo-sapiens," which means "thinking being" and over time has grown to mean "a person that thinks or has a mind." Therefore, man means mind. A man meets the challenges of life and does not compromise his principles because of circumstances or the pressures of his condition, and he cannot be intimidated by other men. His decisions are his own, and yet he is not afraid or shamed and does not consider his seeking the counsel or assistance of either his woman or other men as a sign of personal weakness.

For he understands all too well the principle, if not the proverb: "Iron sharpens iron and one man sharpens another." A man communicates and resolves his differences with other men intelligently. A man admits when he is wrong, out of order, or in error and does not feel himself to be a chump, fool, or sucker in doing so. Men are responsible for their actions and act responsibly. A man will respect another man even though he may dislike him or fails to get along with him. A man manages his life and wealth strategically (with caution). A man respects himself and commands respect from others by the very way he speaks and carries himself. A man is the protector and planner of life. He is a builder and not a destroyer and is the exemplar of strength and stability and a model of behavior for both men and women. He is not a "player" because life is too close to death to play with.

A man works to change his conditions and circumstances, but a boy meekly submits and conforms to them. A man struggles all his life and makes struggle his discipline, his attitude, his way of life. A man will avoid trouble but will not run away from it. A man will work to make present circumstances suit his future needs.

A man is plan oriented and goal oriented, and he checks and constantly renews himself, realizing that life is a continuous growth and is dependent on social interaction, social awareness, and interpersonal relations requiring mutual consultation in decision making. Man (mind) aspires for more and more excellence within himself and his environment, always striving to rise above and to extend himself beyond his present position or situation. A man's greatest obstacle to achieving manhood is his undisciplined self.

I Killed Life with a Dream

July 26, 2013
Age: 32 years old

Staring through my bifocals or my mental mind enhancers.
My mind questions my eyes and the reality it faces,
for my eyes see a reality for which my mind tries to deface, it
doesn't matter how thick the shade the sunlight is still in
my face - in my darkest hour trying to hide from the
moonlight does not take the moonlight away, not wanting
to deal with reality but wanting a reality to create.

I close my eyes to life as it is and look through my mind
beyond what it seems, I killed life with a dream.

Rewind it to the time when a particle from a star fell
from the universe into the atmosphere of my mother's
drink, she sipped, ingested, a seed implanted from an
unknown specimen. I mean, I know who he is, just never
felt the connection... oh lord, I know what I need, just
give me direction...

I thought the gold that glitter was the goal to achieve,
until my neck broke out into a rash, and I'm pretending its
nothing, it's, something that will pass.

I knew what it was I just rather what it projected I had.
I'm being validated. I'm appreciated. I feel a part of
something by those who are just as lost and misguided as
I am – we all need to pull up our pants, but this is my
family, and we all killing life with a dream.

I enrolled in school to further societies idealistic reality
of success and put behind the sights of my mind
wishing thinking. but the lack of finances crippled what
was already a handicapped soul. The lack of guidance

63

is me losing grasp, I had no passion; I was losing my hold.

I was weak.
Lost.
Confused.
Uncertain.

I was shooting for the pipe-dream instead of accepting reality and being happy for being on a team, society deems, preparing oneself for their future because there's no social security in dreams.

I'm educated but not school educated I have no degree,
so no open doors for me. I'm stuck inside this closet
with the key on the floor, on the other side of the door,
watching the shadow from under the door but unable to
reach it, and even if I could, how do I unlock myself from
inside,

how do I unlock what's insides when I'm the one who broke
the key off into the lock and locked myself inside?
Preventing opportunities, I just killed my-self demise,
I put myself in here, I just killed myself alive.

How do I relate to a world who sees my struggles as a brick wall of bad choices? Influenced by what was in front of me - blamed for what wasn't.

I bang on the door with both hands and all my might.
Can anybody hear me?
Can anybody hear me?
Does anybody freaking hear me?

My mind sees a life where doubts has now taken the place of potential. Where begging has now taken the place of what I thought was given. I'm pleading with tears to an unknown God to give me a chance to prove myself, when all I do is load the gun and refuse to fire. In the mirror practicing aim, taking make believe shots wishing someone will see what my ego thought was greatness. What I thought was potential has now been replaced with asking for your sympathy, to understand what I been through. When it was always me, killing my life with a dream.

From wanting to be a rapper,
before that thinking I can sing,
nobody being honest with me except time that took wise to come onto the scene. So, forget all of you who added to me living life as a dream.

As I look through my bifocals, I deemed this unknown potential a fact, when I'm really a risk, not an investment more of a liability in a sense. Is this fear you hear? Is this me in contempt? I'm just writing what i feel.
This is how I feel.

While everybody is traveling, having kids and doing fun things. Taking city tests as their plan A as I chase what their fear won't allow them to be with no plan B's, even though they no plans to seed. Just to be a part of a pyramid scheme they will never get to the top of the rock to see - they're living life, no dream, empty, but content and free. I want to be just like them and a part of them wishes to be just like me.

As I take the bifocals off my mind and deal with what's in front of my eyes I see, I walk dead in sight as fear whispers old man, you're too young to be killing life with a dream. Now I'm taking the same city tests in efforts to save some of this life I have left man screw this dream.

If I become nothing my kids become whatever.
And not only will they blame my eyes for not being in their lives, not giving them the opportunity for their minds to see me strive, their lack of understanding will turn my efforts to lies, my arrogance becomes their ignorance, my selfishness becomes their pride.

They blame the dream I chased unsuccessfully for the reason they are where they are in their lives. I killed my life with a dream and in death I continue to kill lives, as my neglected non-watered seeds die in a drought from a life, I dreamed.

Thinking if I don't walk in the light of who I see myself to be, then I'm covered in the shadows of who I don't want to see myself to be, even if it is what God wants me to be. It doesn't make it a reality my mind wants to believe.

But when my being no longer walks this Earth, and have not achieved the things I dreamed,
wasted my whole life investing in death,
trying to give life to a dream. Deep down I know somehow,
whether recognize for great or peril,
what to do or not to do,
forever,
in some shape form or fashion, I will live on through my words.

Finally,
unconsciously,
In death, I will live life from a dream.
Because a life lost in a dream, gives life to a dream.
I may have killed my life with a dream,
but I give life to yours. I love you.

The Way He Drives

February 2, 2012
Age: 31

Is the way you drive a reflection of who you are? Can the way you drive serve as a depiction representing the many character traits that bottles the makings of you? Is the aggression of a driver who as a person is coy, the lion in the cage released from its unconscious purgatory? Would it be okay to say that if the way you drive, is the opposite of the kind of individual you are, that a therapist should look at it as a tool to diagnose, advise, and treat you. All theory, of course.

I have known my best friend all of his life. He's the most genuine man I know, flawed only in the average everyday imperfections of a young adult man. I have noticed the aggression he lacks in life appears while he is behind the wheel of a car. Maybe because he has 100 percent control and there isn't a fear of the unknown. This isn't up for debate; it's just my opinion from an observational standpoint. He's your rough and rugged kind of man and doesn't keep a clean car. He's not too big in the smooth department but makes up for it with his intelligence and undeniable logic. So, it doesn't surprise me that he handles the road in the same fashion, rough and rugged, without an ounce of smoothness.

He is known by many to be selfish, or what he likes to call "self-preservation." Either way, he drives like he's the only one on the road. With every acceleration he seems to be racing to a finish line with no destination. His need for speed represents his yearning for adventure, for life, to break up the monotony. Now what if he attacked life with the same type of aggression, with the same amount of fearlessness? Would it change the way he drives? I highly doubt it, but one must consider the fact that who we are appears in the many things we do.

He is not patient at all, so it is also not surprising that in the wee hours of the morning he runs the red lights because he knows nobody is watching. He takes that chance, that risk, knowing his actions can lead to unwanted consequence. He doesn't take chances or risks in life, so why does he take them here? And if he were to incorporate who he is as a person on the road, I believe it would make him a better driver. So basically, the connection between who you are and how you drive can go both ways.

He's not a confident man and in many ways unsure of himself, but on the road, you wouldn't believe that. Something about that power and control, that know-how and skill behind the wheel, propels a confidence in him I wish could rollover into his life. But it's quite the opposite. But of course, any man would have confidence and be sure of himself when he possesses the skills he has on the road. It's like putting a gun in the hand of a man with motive. He feels like most of the people driving need to be walking. On screen, he's Jerry McGuire, but off he's Cuba Gooding Jr.

Now if the way you drive does in some way describes who you are, it's safe to say that it says who you aren't as well. Maybe I'm digging too deep into it. I haven't done any research, so there isn't anything to base this theory on, no case study in a sense, just my opinion on what I know about a person and how that person drives. But I do believe that the way he drives represents in many ways who he is and who he isn't. Or maybe I'm just wrong, and it is just the way he drives.

Yes, I Am Your Friend. I Just ...

June 7, 2012
Age: 31

There was a situation where I allowed my emotions to compel me to act violently which wasn't in the best interest of myself, my friend and our relationship. In this situation my friend was put in a position where he had to decide to be loyal to me or himself and his family. As a friend I must understand that I can't put us in a situation that would question our friendship. And if he decides to put himself and his family first, how can I be mad at that.

My friend is more cerebral then I am, and this creates the balance. I'm much more emotional than he is, but our connection is of common intellect. I'm the hothead who lashes out and he serves as a mediator who has talked us out of many fights. But this one night he couldn't talk us out of it. He had a very important job interview the next day and decided to call the cops on me because I wouldn't calm down and he seen where it was heading. He went home shortly after to his family.

I took a bad beaten before the cops arrived, but we were all arrested and spent a night in jail. I put my friend in a position on whether he should have my back or not. Having my back means jeopardizing his freedom and livelihood for the right to say he was loyal. He made the right decision. In my opinion he was a friend. His decision showed where his priorities were and how he valued himself. It had nothing to do with his loyalty nor friendship to me. He was a man who protected his family first and that's important.

He said he felt bad after because he felt like he had let me down, that he wasn't a friend and had my back. I quickly told him, "You did have my back. Because I don't know how I would have felt knowing I ruined your employment opportunities because my drinking and acting out violently. You saved me from hurting you at the expense of one night in jail. I rather that than the burden of you missing out on your dream. You feel bad because you do love me and want to be there for me. Feeling bad does not mean you did not make the right decision. It just means your human and its human nature to want to be there for the person you love. So, never question your loyalty. I know you're my friend, it's just..."

My Journey Up North: The Infirmary

January 24, 2007
Age: 26

"We called you down here because the X-rays we took of your lungs last month are showing a problem. We're not quite sure what it is. Do you smoke?"

"No."

"Are you having any night sweats, any loss of weight?"

"No."

"Are you coughing uncontrollably?"

"No, I feel fine."

"We're going have to do a cytology, which is the study of cells, to see if there's any abnormality in your lungs that is causing what appears to be fluid to leak in."

My eyes enlarged as she finished her sentence. "What are you saying, besides the obvious? What, what fluid?"

"Something is causing fluid to leak into your lungs, and at this moment, we don't know if it's cancerous or not. So, for the next three days we are going to take samples of your mucus. We are going to need you to sign this release form. This gives us the permission, granted by you, to take you to an outside hospital in the event any procedures need to be done to get a further understanding of what we have going on here. At this time, I would like for to go back to your dorm and gather all your belongings and come back. We have to admit you into isolation from general population until all contagions are ruled out."

"Contagions like what?" I quickly asked.

"Tuberculosis."

"I thought the TB results came back negative."

"Yes, it did. But at this point we must factor in all possibilities, despite lab results, just to be positive. I know this is all happening fast, but we'll get to the bottom of this, okay?"

"Okay, Nurse."

Wow. Cancerous? Cancerous? That's all I heard over and over in my head. It's like nothing is getting better. Cancer. I struggled all my life to be who I am and follow what is only in my heart just to come to jail and find out there might be a chance I have cancer. What's the worth of life if all that is achieved is nothing?

It's Been 5 Weeks

Journal Entry
November 14, 2012
Age: 31

It sucks that my thirty-second birthday is coming in about two weeks because I don't need to be thinking about getting older. I'm contemplating whether I should even add what I'm going through right now to this book because it's embarrassing. Being back at my mother's place and staying at my girlfriend's house makes it real hard to sleep at night. I can just imagine what people think of me.

Watching all my friends and peers on Facebook with their kids smiling and content, hurts my heart too, because I'm not being the father, I always thought I would be. I'm just money every week and broken promises. I must keep writing and keep striving to be happy with myself so I'm not this bitter old unfulfilled man.

I really hate that the women get to make the last decision on whether to bring a child into this world or not. Because no matter how much I begged and pleaded with this girl that I wasn't ready, she did what she wanted to do. I know I should have not had unprotected sex and that I am just as responsible. And this is not to say I don't love my daughter. But she deserves better.

Bringing a child into this world is supposed to be an agreement between both the man and the woman. At the time, I was living in my mother's basement, a year out of jail with nothing going on but this pipe dream of becoming a writer and it was a terrible time. I know I'm all over the place right now and sounding bitter towards my daughter's mother. I just see myself continuing the same cycle I vowed to end. I'm putting my needs first and my excuse is that I've been chasing this person I've been chasing for too long. I can't stop now, for no one, not even my own flesh and blood. Now I sound like my selfish ass mother.

Nothing is right at this moment. I don't feel like a man, damn sure not getting the best dad award and I'm having a hard time arranging this book. Is it autobiography? A book of literary collections? What's the theme? What's the market and demographic? Will putting numerous pieces spanning over 13 years in non-chronological tell the story I'm trying to tell? Will it all make sense?

I'm second- guessing this book right now. Every time I sit down and go over it, it just feels like something is missing, like it could be better. But what else am I going to do? I can't just quit. If I don't finish this book, am I who I think I am?

Separating Reality from Wishful Thinking

January 29, 2007
Age: 27

The reality of the matter is that I committed a crime and the city of New York has given the state a date to release me, a date I come home. Wishful thinking is the possibility that I may come home sooner. I believe I am immensely talented, with the potential to do things of paramount proportions. That's the reality. Now being the billionaire I want to be is wishful thinking. I'm not saying it can't happen, but based on my current situation, its far-fetched.

Sometimes our wishful thinking can lead us right into a brick wall of what some call failure, and another brick wall, and another one, until we give up and deal with reality. They say a goal without a plan is simply a wish. But what if your plan to reach your goal is nothing but a bunch of unrealistic wishful thoughts? What then? How do you know if you're caught up in the imaginative world of wishful thinking? How do you know when you're in too deep? How do you separate reality from wishful thinking when you're trying to make those wishes a reality?

I guess you must look at your odds and weigh the pros and cons. Is wishful thinking bad or does it give us fuel to continue burning? Is the fact that I'm not the only one who sees my vision make it real and not a delusion? Am I wishful thinking now to ease the pain of my reality? Because reality is and specifically states that I'm a criminal, a convicted felon with no promise today to become anything more than what my rap sheet projects. So, who am I? I could have been anybody I wanted to be, a lawyer, doctor, or an executive at a fortune 500 company somewhere in the field of marketing with good pay and benefits. Maybe I wouldn't have gone through so many struggles, especially the struggle that comes with chasing wishful thoughts of being one of the biggest rappers in the music industry. Maybe I wouldn't have put my family through so much if I'd just dealt with reality and followed society. Am I cursed? Am I trying to get to a world that only exists in my head? Am I rebelling against society for the simple pleasures of the moment and not the stability of tomorrow? Am I a sad case of hope with no glory? Will I be one of those old men in life who does nothing but achieves failure?

Where did this frame of mind come from? Am I basing my wants in life from a realistic skill and ability or from just potential? Are my dreams and aspirations simply a figment of my imagination? I mean, people with my talent and nowhere near my talent have made it. How did they make it? How do I know if I'm living in a fantasy or not? How do I know that the life I want is not the life I need? What is my purpose? How do I make sense of it in my head if it isn't in my heart?

Maybe if I keep trying, I'll find out. Or maybe if I turn away now there won't be any more suffering and I can find out as well. But will I be happy if I turn away? Will I be at peace with myself? Is turning away the reality I need to face to cure me from this wishful thinking, to cure me from me, from being my own enemy? I was chasing a music career recklessly. And maybe I was the only one who believed it could happen. I'm realizing now that people were indirectly saying I wasn't any good. I was always complimented on my writing ability but never my music. So, the question now is, without music, what do I do? What's my reality when the dream is no more?

76   RANDOM THOUGHTS

Koala Bear Sun

A Journey to Reach Spiritual Enlightenment, Part 1
March 9, 2008
Age: 27

Allow me to reintroduce myself. I am no longer Jamai Wray. My Buddhist name is Koala Bear Sun. As I write to you from where some would call prison, which is known to me as straight from the slums of the Shaolin Temple of Zen Zen Zah. I have become one with myself and I one with the wind. Usually at this time, I will be deep in the realms of one's spirit, sipping on herbal tea of the Secret Golden Flower. The fresh mountain air has released the true essence of oneself, revealing my true being. I am a rat. In my past life, Sam-su-ru, which is the circle of death, birth, and rebirth in Buddhism, inspired my present form, this vessel of flesh everybody has come to know. So, as I begin to reminisce on my first life, I step out of the circle of that realm and into the conscious realm of intelligence with hopes of acquiring spiritual enlightenment. (Hmmmmmm, may the vibrations reach you.)

It all started with my first excursion into the Cambodian jungle in search of the upalytic tree of the monkey spirit. My first master, Bamboo King of the Congo Forest, has transformed my traditional foundation of psychological time of the past and future into the alertness of the present moment, allowing me the privilege to have Power of the Now. I am no longer a slave to my evil thoughts and bad memories, a slave to the chronological meltdown of mind and body. I move on a higher level of consciousness. I realized that there is a vast realm of spirituality I must encounter to be truly enlightened beyond this world to live forever. I now know what truly matters in life. My next escapade will be into the mountains of Tibet, in search of the Temple of the Invisible Fist, to empower my natural ninja techniques and methods of vanishing the mind. There I will find the Leaf of Bruce Lee, a rare cannabis that grows once every thousand years.

Now that I've risen above thought, I can finally breathe the air of spirituality. And in time I will be able to move in between dimensions at any given time. I know this may seem hard to believe. That's because you're using your mind to try to comprehend my words. The mind, which feeds off the ego, will not interpret the essence of this truth in its entirety.

My master, Long Trunk of the Mandingo, has the herbal seed of Zim-bu-do (do-do-ya), which was originally only found in the mountains of the Himalaya where the true player of Zen was born. This tea, Zim-bu-do (do-do-ya), triggers the brain's memory of fear by isolating the imagination as well as heightening the Angola, which is responsible for creativity, and opens a door in time by using brain waves that match the cosmic rays of the universe. The first time I tried it I ended up on top of Mount Everest with a kufi on and a Bible in my hand, screaming, "I don't believe in God." Don't ask.

My master, Sho-nuff Dragonfoot of Harlem told me that you must use creative visualization before you take flight of the navigator in between dimensions. I hope you take this serious because I've really given my unconsciousness over to the spiritual world. I didn't realize the insanity of my actions until I freed my thoughts from my ego. But don't listen to my words. Look beyond them. Rise above my text if you are unable to look beyond it. It is only a vessel used to convey my thoughts and cannot recognize the reality to which my words point. If you can't, then disregard everything I just said and continue to make the face you're making. But before I'm released, I will be a Master. I will go by the name of Master Koala Bear Sun of Higher Consciousness beyond the Mind and Thought of Self. I know that's a long name, but I would have deserved it. I shaved every piece of hair from my body and I only eat dry oatmeal. I'll be home soon.

I must go now. The wind is calling me. (Hmmmmmm, may the vibrations reach you.)

To be continued.

Baby Jesus

November 11, 2011
Age: 30

My girl is with child and being that I hold myself very high on a pedestal, I've been telling her that we're about to bring baby Jesus back. I don't know why in the lords name I told her that because now she really thinks she's Mary and that she's carrying baby Jesus. She's buying sandals, little toolboxes, and baby work belts; the baby shower looked like a flea market for carpenters. Then she turned around and got mad and called me cheap because I chose to build the bassinet instead of buying one. I thought it was about being frugal, right?

We argue, of course. What couple doesn't? I'm pretty sure Mary and Joseph got into it. I'm pretty sure Joseph was like, look, I don't give two goats and a lamb if you are carrying baby Jesus, I'm going down to Barns & Nobles for a drink, and that's that. Now just imagine for a second what Joseph really went through. I mean, how do you tell your boys your wife is carrying another man's baby, and God's baby at that? The Bible wasn't even in circulation, and God didn't really get famous like that until Jesus came along. So how do you tell your boys that she's pregnant by some mystical being that lives in the clouds? Just imagine a drunk Joseph coming home every night from the Barn after getting joked on by his boys and trying to be supportive. It had to be hell for that man.

We just got engaged not too long ago too. I remember the first time I went to her place. I'll never forget it because I became a huge skeptic after that. We were in her bedroom and I looked over and saw that her pillows looked like they had been in family for three generations, passed down with stories behind them and all, just rough looking. To this day, she still brings up whenever we argue about my buying her pillows for her birthday. I mean, I had only known her for three months, but I didn't see the problem. She needed them.

And why do women that are in a relationship but not married say "my husband." Seriously, do females do that trying to send energy out, hoping one day he proposes? Are you trying to be a part of some secret society that opposes single women? Is it peer pressure? Or could it be those darn Disney movies you watched as a little girl, when you thought you were Princess Jasmine or Cinderella? I blame Disney. Disney screwed up females' heads, getting their hopes high with this marriage thing at an early age. All this pressure and drama they put up with before they get married just to divorce you once you get caught sending a text message to another woman. Like really?

And I would like to thank my fiancée's father too. He choreographed everything for her when we first met. See, I was only home from prison for like three weeks when we met, and she volunteered that information to him. He in return gave her some advice that almost made her lose her freaking mind. He told her to fall back and let me be. Don't pressure me into anything. He's been in jail for a few years, so don't overcrowd him. Give him space.

No man wants to feel locked down in a cage, especially when he's just coming home from one. He told her I was going to do things she, or any woman, may not approve of. But if she really liked me and saw potential in me, then she needed to give me time and let me grow into her. Let me roam, let me be, and if it was to be, it would be. Don't force anything because she was only going to push me away. Some real stupid advice if you ask me. I would never tell my daughter anything like this.

But for nearly two years, that's exactly what she did, and now we're happily engaged and expecting a baby, with psychiatrist fees up our tail because every little freaking thing I do I'm cheating. If I'm not where she thinks I should be based on her GPS coordinates and satellite readings, I'm cheating. If I don't answer the phone when she calls me and don't call right back, I'm cheating. If I'm texting a friend or just touching my phone period, I'm cheating. I can't do regular normal activities without her thinking I'm cheating or plotting to cheat.

I'm going over our budget, you know, got the pen in my mouth, glasses on, calculator, I'm crunching numbers and everything and she thinks I'm putting together how many females I can get away with seeing, when, and where to meet them. If I spend this much time with this one, that will subtract the cost ratio with this one. If I sell Monica stock, I can buy more shares of Penny If I cut back on Rachel, I can go to the strip club more. Blah blah blah. Just crazy. It's like being in jail.

I talk about my lady a lot because I'm in that phase where I'm still trying to figure all this being in love, monogamous relationship, commitment, being with only one woman for the rest of my life and I'm only twenty-five, marriage, beer bellies, going bald, Sports Center once a week, hanging out with other married people stuff out, and I'm really starting to believe that I'm not cut out for all this commitment **stuff**.

I'm truly starting to think that I don't have what it takes to be in a relationship with one woman. I'm really starting to believe that I just proposed to her because she was pregnant, and I don't want this innocent child to grow up in a broken home like I did and be taken to child support.

So, I'm just here for the sake of this child when I really don't want to be here at all. But why else would a woman who the doctors said couldn't have children get pregnant if she wasn't indeed carrying baby Jesus. I'm going down to Barns & Nobles. I need a drink.

My Journey Up North: Isolation, Day 1

January 25, 2007

Age: 26

"Good morning, Mr. Wray, how are we feeling?" asks the nurse."

"Other than the fact that I'm surrounded by a bunch of white people in a small town I never heard of labeled an enemy of the state and oblivious to what's going on with my health, I feel great."

"A little bit of too much information. Any shortness of breath? Any coughing up blood?"

"No, why would I be coughing up blood?"

"Well, the reason you're here is because your X-ray's are crappy, and there's a slight possibility you may have tuberculosis. Those are the symptoms."

"So did the results come back from the mucus samples yet?" "No, we're still waiting. Have you smoked in the past or do you smoke?"

"Well, it's been six years since I smoked cigarettes, but I still smoke marijuana."

"Any hard stuff, like crack?"

"No, I don't smoke crack. Do you?"

"No, why would you ask me a question like that?"

"The same reason you asked me. I want to know for medical purposes."

"Okay then, blood pressure is normal as well as your temperature. I'll come check on you later. Is there anything I can get you?"

"Yes, a pen and paper please."

"A pencil and some paper coming right up."

I know her asking those questions was procedure, but so what. I was offended. As I rest my head on my pillow with the words "cancer" and "tuberculosis" floating around in my head, I start to think about my mother and how depressed she already is. I am her first born son. My being locked away must be very embarrassing for her. I know this would probably drive her crazy. I hope whatever it is, it can be cured. To be closer to death than my dream, to be far from home in a time of need, only weakens my efforts and kills all hope. This shit is really crazy.

The Cause and Effect (What If)

May 10, 2007
Age: 26

I have so much to give, so much to do, so much to be
if I give up now, there will be no more of me.
Giving up is like death, a shot that killed my body of
work, if I give up now, I'd just be a body of a convict,
a statistical blurt, mommy, it hurts.
So, who is this man that stands alone and only feels at
home with words,
who no one seems to know, who I don't seem to know,
who can't move forward because I have to move back, to
my mother's home?
So, do I try something else? Is she delusional?
She being my aunt who sees my being achieving things
greater than I ever could conceive.
If I keep going, will it be?
Could success be a reality or is she just wishful when she
thinks, is it me?
Am I my own enemy that imprisons myself in this bubble
of fear, waiting and not making my turn, making excuses
that blames my surroundings for the reason I'm
unaccomplished, what is it? What's wrong with me? Why do
my failures outshine my accomplishments?
Why do I have this feeling that I'm not going to accomplish it,
be a part of it,
and just be another sad love song with the potential but don't
form a bond with it? So, for me to realize the realism of
this reality I must be able to see the fruits of my labor,
so my giving up ever is practically incapable—my giving
up this is the cause that will affect me
at fifty years old writing poems, what … what if?

Whether you feed your mind or not,
whether you do something to fill that void or lay idle,
whether you don't try to fill that emptiness that
comes with not knowing your purpose or do,
who you will become is inevitable.
—Jamai Wray

A Cold Night in December

Journal Entry
December 19, 2012
Age: 32

Here I am again, stranded. Mother is not home, brother is not at his place, and now I'm contemplating a hotel until I go to work, but I don't want to spend the money. Save money to put the book out and get a one-bedroom apartment is the goal, but nights like this make me want to give in and just get a room.

Numerous times I almost cracked and gave up over copious arguments with my mother, forgetting I'm under her roof. Forgetting that no matter how old I am she will always treat me like a child, especially since I don't have my own. The worst feeling in the world at this moment is not getting the respect your age demands, but the respect of the position you're in. It's crazy cold out here, and once again I'm hit with a dose of my reality. I'm homeless. That's my position.

My Journey Up North: Isolation, Day 25

February 18, 2007
Age: 26

The nurse came in with some good news; cancer came back negative. Which is good. It seems like they're working from the worst-case scenario down. Whatever it is, I'm just hoping it's nothing life-threatening.

The last couple of days and yesterday in particular have been very scary. Whenever I lay down at night, I start coughing uncontrollably. Yesterday, in the middle of the day, I was lying down, and this funny-tasting liquid came up. Now I had tasted this unusual and unfamiliar taste before, but never did it come up like this. So, as I was coughing, I went over to the toilet to spit and couldn't believe my eyes. My saliva was mixed with blood. Which answers the question the nurse asked twenty-four days ago? Whatever is going on is getting worse.

"Is everything okay in there?" The nurse knocks on the window.

I shake my head no in response.

She puts on her mask and enters the room. "What seems to be the problem?"

"I just coughed up blood."
"Was the whole thing blood or was it mixed in with your saliva?" she says.

"It was mixed."

"Then most likely it's not from your chest. It can be a broken blood vessel in your throat or from your sinuses."

She went to get a jar to put my saliva in so they could take it back to the lab and determine where the blood did come from.

"Don't worry, Mr. Wray. You'll live to write another day."

Whatever is going on inside my lungs is progressing.

Love and in Love With?

August 2, 2010
Age: 29

How do I live the rest of my life with you in my head? How do I lie next to the one I say I love, thinking about the one I'm in love with, grasping her frame with the image of you cascading over my thoughts? What if I didn't blame God for putting everything in the way of our love? What if you didn't live in another state and didn't have a baby on the way? What if I didn't lie with the intention to protect your feelings and my image? I mean, I'm really who I say I am. I'm just going through some things. I assume you wouldn't understand and would judge me for ultimately affecting your decision to continue to talk to me. What if I gave you that chance? What if I fought hand and knees, blood, sweat, and tears for what I felt in my soul instead of entertaining thoughts of the obvious? Convincing my mind, which eventually won over my heart, to believe a lie, a lie full of conveniences, a lie conceived from fear, a lie that brought forth so many truths. For how long can I live with the lie my mind made my heart believe as it slowly eats at the very essence of my spirit? Hoping that your being out of sight can rid you from my mind.

How could I give up on what I feel is the most significant ability God has given us, the ability to love, to give ourselves effortlessly to another soul? To say you love someone means you care about her welfare in the arms of selflessness, but is my love for you really love or just an addictive clinging created by redundant acts of what is perceived to be love? Does being in love allow someone to come in and steal your heart or create the overwhelming thought of losing you that's so unbearable it outweighs any novelty of someone else? I would love to know the contrast between love and being in love, and does it really exist? Are they opposites?

Is it real? What does being in love really mean past the word and why does it have so much power? Why do we put up with the worst while wishing for the best? Do we trick ourselves by using this word to exemplify how we feel? Does saying I'm in love make you, me, us seem more seriously devoted to the mere fact that we have a few things in common, that we enjoy each other's company, and can deal with each other flaws? Is it just the novelty of this new found love, so fresh and vibrant, we call being in love when it's really just a word with a euphoric effect that allows us to love more convincingly until I get tired of you, you get tired of me, and that being in love feeling that felt so real depreciates?

Does being in love appreciate? Does it appreciate beyond the measures of worth that even in those moments of doubt and fatigue hope is just a refresh button away? Is love like fine wine that only tastes good when aged? Is the man or woman you're with today just there to prepare you for the next one, giving you the priceless experience of knowing yourself and the opposite sex so that when your soul mate does eventually come along it doesn't take a lifetime to realize it?

Just appreciate life and its lessons, please; many don't get the chance to love. If you are in love, is it possible to fall out? Will the person who has your heart make it impossible for another one to have it? I say I'm in love with someone else, but I'm with the one I love. So am I the typical man that doesn't know what he wants, is scared of what he feels is real, thinks he could do better, and settles for the sake of conveniences, or am I just a victim of not being loved, so I don't know how to love or recognize it when it's there? Sabotaging my chance of true love because it's just too good to be true, I say. Allowing others' opinions on what I do and choose to affect what feels so real. This love thing is so confusing. For t h e life of me, I don't understand why people toss the word love around so carelessly.

Why do women allow that word to dictate and summarize what should be looked for in action? I guess it's just the feeling of being wanted, that transparent blanket of security people needs to feel alive and have purpose.

As I lie next to the one I say I love thinking about the one I'm in love with, I wonder if I will ever love the one I say I love like I love you. To love and be in love, that's the question, a question that doesn't necessarily have an answer, an answer that may not be looked at for its unique interpretation of one's moral comprehension, for each person's definition of love and being in love is different. Loving your mother and loving your wife are two different types of love. Let that serve as the template for now because, in my opinion, to love and be in love with is just as both powerless and useless as the words *sorry* and *friend*. So, what's love?

The Definition of Love

September 25, 2012
Age: 31

A man who says a woman will never understand how a man can be in love and still cheat doesn't know what true love is. Love doesn't justify its actions with matters of the flesh. For love is not ignorance. Love is not breaking a woman's heart repeatedly, for love is not hurt. Love is not pain. Love doesn't surprise you with infidelity, for love is not deceit. Love is not selfish. Love doesn't creep into the bed in the middle of the night or knock at your door with a secret love affair. There's no password or anything to hide with love. Love is not condescending. Love doesn't suffer from inferiority complexes but of equality, for love is whole.

Love is not sleeping around with your child's mother or father or anyone for that matter but claim your love rests solely with your significant other. It is obvious that person is not significant at all. For love is honor. Love is respect. Love is discipline; love is self-control. You don't risk an eternity of love and happiness for a moment of pleasure; that's not love. Love is not a moment or season but a lifetime. If you are not ready to commit your all, then be honest. Settling down is not something you figure out mentally, but a certainty you feel in your heart and soul to be faithful and committed not just to your loved one, but to yourself. You must love yourself enough, to love.

In order to truly be in love, there must be that excitement. For love is joy and drive; love is hunger and that thirsty thought quenched by desires, knowing she's the first thing on your mind in the morning and the last thing on your mind at night. Love is security; love is sacrifice.

Love is confidence in a bond. Love is bragging rights. Love is confirmation. Love is knowing what needs to be done and fixing it. Love is surviving storms, for love is withstanding. When it comes to somebody else's heart, you must first understand where yours have been, where it's at now, and where you want it to be. Love is loving you.

Love is responsibility and for many the wrong choice of word. Love is not excuses. Do unto others as you want others to do unto you. If the fear of losing the one you claim you love doesn't outweigh the novelty of something different, then love is not what you have. Love is deeper than its perception, for many men lack understanding of what true love is. Love is fear. To love a woman and to be faithful to her, for men, takes time and experience. You must be completely free from your ego. You must be disciplined. To love not in word or theory, but in action. Love is romance, flowers just because. Love is patience and endurance. A man understands his power and responsibility and knows that breaking a woman down only continues the cycle of mental poison that rolls over to our little girls and little boys. I want my daughter to recognize what true love is, but first I must show her. I must be an example. Most of the men who grew up in broken homes without their fathers and even the ones who had their fathers, were not taught what it is to be a man because their fathers had no clue themselves. Love is understanding.

Love is jealously, for without it, there's no love. Love will scare you to death because you can feel how vulnerable you are and how crushed you would be if anything were to happen to your significant other. Love is a contradiction, for love can be pain. This definition of what I call love is not something you can pick up in a book and find its meaning or similarities, for love spills from your heart. This is a feeling I feel and share with my lady, this my definition of love.

Love in Battle

May 29, 2012
Age: 31

A thorn from her rose lips
Wounded by loves fist
Captured by the blissful impression of promise on the
battlefield where death came from a kiss.
Poison is self-inflicted into the veins, guided by the compass of
two hearts' lack of direction.
Rushed into battle, blinded by the beauty of victory, we stand
together, alone.
Uncertain and unprotected
as hopeless thoughts linger in our subconscious, masked by
rhetoric of optimism.
This may be our last battle, for a future of promise is ruined by
what we accepted and scarred by fear.
A scar that will always remain no matter how good the
wounds may heal and how hopeful we are of what we want
to expect. As we lay down our shields and remove our armor
to break from war, deep down we really want to define
incessant.
For whatever grounds our feet shall travel, let's not allow
space and separation to create doubt, for we are still
everything we want. It is not you.
It is me,
and the arrogance of my ignorant and undisciplined self.

Confessions of a Wounded Ego in Love

Age: 31

Letter 1: Damage Control
May 12, 2012

I woke up this morning not surprised by my first thought, for it was of you. I feel better than I did a couple of days ago and more optimistic as I move forward. I pray the energy I send with just a click of the share button is well received and sent back, giving me hope as I attempt damage control.

I never told a lie until I fell in love with you. I convinced my mind to believe it was to protect you, but in return, keeping you in the dark only shattered what armor I assumed secrecy would conceal. Yes, I cheated on you and betrayed your trust. Yes, I lied trying to buy time to fix my situation because losing you was not an option. Yes, I felt I was slick enough and wouldn't get caught. Yes, I thought by not telling my baby mother about us and keeping her happy to keep our relationship at peace, that I could manage to love you and be successful, but all I did was put myself into a hole.

I was riding high on my ego. The same ego that is wounded in your absence. It's said that you never get things right until you mess it up a few times; that's what makes achieving your goal more precious. Knowing you worked for it and that it didn't come easy is the recipe of content. Like I said once before, I'd rather lose trying, than give no effort in defeat.

Letter 2: Getting to Know the Presumptive Damage Control Candidate
May 14, 2012

I love you—mere words carelessly thrown around sometimes by people who used it to express a feeling that action can say better. So from this day forward, I will lock those words away inside my vault until I feel my action supersedes mere rhetoric, making the moment I gracefully rub my hand down your face and utter those words again, equivocal to what you see, to what you feel.

From as far back as I can remember, I've only loved myself. I've only had to prove to myself how much I cared. I never thought a broken heart at sixteen would affect me as a man. I never thought a loveless mother choosing her wants and needs over me would affect me as a man. I never thought I would unconsciously continue the cycle, even when I consciously vowed not to.

For years, I focused on the things that made me happy because I was the only one to please, the only one who knew and cared to. Yes, I am a victim of my circumstances, but do not mistake this plea as an excuse to get your sympathy. As I sit in this milk truck thinking about my flaws and defects, I only hope your faith is stronger, enabling love not to give up on love.

Last night I told the truth when I said I'd never been in love like this. I never cared for anyone but myself and dealt with mainly ego. I wasn't taught how to treat and love a woman. Not having you will hurt me more in the long run than busting my ass in the moment for what seems impossible. But to call it quits, to erase you from my phone, to delete your pictures, to act like I don't care doesn't supersede how good it feels to be with you. That's what I'm fighting for. You're not cursed, just in love, and being in love isn't easy, never was, or ever will be.

98

I'm running for the highest office in your land. I want to be the president of your heart. I'm Jamai Wray, and I hope you approve this message.

Letter 3: The Reason I'm Running for Your Office
May 15, 2012

Life feels so weird without you. It feels incomplete, purposeless, and awkward. It's as if you were meant to be in my clutch. I want to take this time to let your heart know that I'm running for the highest seat in your land. I'm running for your office. Having just the thought of hope in this moment is better than having a whole mind of regrets in the past. You're special in so many indescribable ways. To cheat love with rhetoric wouldn't be real so excuse me if it comes off that way.

The first thing we do every time we approach each other after days without is smile. We're happy. You know it. I know it. And I dread the thought of what it would feel like to say how good I had it when it's gone. I want to prove I can be a man and take on the responsibility of caring for you, supporting you, and giving you the security and comfort every woman deserves. I don't want to waste your time. I want you to depend on my decisions. And even though my record doesn't show the accuracy usually expected from a presidential hopeful, I want you to follow your heart and say, yes, we can. Yes, we can.

I truly believe from all my screw ups that I know what it takes to make sure my first lady is secure when she's dealing with a man who's been emotionally unstable, thoughtless, selfish, and many other piggish attributes. As I stand before you in this e- mail, I say fight with me. Take my hand and fight for what your mind doesn't want your heart to follow. Fight with me, babes, please.

Letter 4: Commencement Speech as I Lay
May 17, 2012

I was always taught to fight for what I believe in, no matter how many times it can be discouraging. My experiences in life thus far, for this position, some would consider to be inadequate. I am an underachiever. How can he be president of your heart, when he's never given anybody his, when he can't see past his self-absorbed cynical self, to care for someone more than he cares about himself? Even as I explain and express my love, it's still hard to be considered genuine and truthful past the punch lines and creative humor used to draw an analogy to what is considered high and worthy. Even in truth, I'm still looked at as not being remorseful, but I'd rather deal with the pain with you here like this and let my delusion keep me hopeful than deal with the pain of your absence and the reality of what follows.

I lay here thinking about you. I mean really, really thinking about you, and there's a part deep inside of me that's really scared of losing you. As I try to find what it is about you that has me so attached, I can't help but to think about how lucky I am. We all deserve the best companion, but sometimes I wonder how I got so lucky. Why is the universe being this good to me? Who or what is watching over me to deliver me this opportunity to love a soul as unblemished as yours? Who knows me enough to consider me worthy? Is this real? Your innocence makes it impossible to ever betray you again. You're the closest thing to perfect I've had the privilege to say I love. During our domestic disagreement, I couldn't do what I would normally do, and that's to act like I don't care if you left, because I do. No longer can I be a victim of my pride. I may not know what it is to be in a real grownup relationship; infancy may continue to show, but I ask you to teach me.

There's a lot I don't know. I've lived a lifestyle where I've been neglected of knowing what it is to love and respect a woman, but I'm learning every day just by your presence. If you're by my side, the pieces of my puzzle will continue to come forth to complete the map whose incompletion led me to you.

I love you, and as I lay across my bed writing my thoughts down, I hope that one day we can get it back to where it was. I know there's a lot of work to do and holes to dig out of as I try to rebuild our economy; but I promise this presidency will be one that our world will remember and be talked about until the end of time.

Shakespearean Love in Battle

June 11, 2012
Age: 31

Jamie
Oh, ye of little faith, do ye not know me to say love has never been my life? I dare your courage to conjure up the audacity to allow your fingers to write such fallacious remarks. They shall dine in hell for perjury, for my love is beyond trends; I am thy craftsman of romance with words of chivalry that are euphonious when heard and delectable when read. If it's war you want, then war is what you will get. I dare ye.

Alice
O how thou loathe in one's unproven ability to win with plausible rhetoric. With these words I thee wed, preposterous. You will not win a battle nor a war with just words, for action speaks louder. It's funny how thou feel the rightly chosen words can replace what needs to be fought for. You wouldn't last a minute in battle, for you know not what you fight for.

Jamie
It's an ugly beauty to watch your brain and heart battle for position, to see your intelligence and logic and pride outwit that big old heart of yours. Asking myself if I played a part in the reason, you're at war with yourself not only baffles me but grabs me more. So much fight, so much anger, so much fear of wanting to love me forces you to conjure excuses on why you assume I don't. But the faith in my heart cannot beat the pride of mind, no matter how much your intelligence and ego tell me I will lose.

No matter how much you defend yourself and put this wall over your heart and pretend like you lay your sword down to give up on the only thing that makes you complete will never win me. Fight with me. Let ye love spark the fight back in you. What do you have to lose?

Alice
You're a pitiful silly man to say I'm at war with myself. For thou not knoweth who he is to say who I am. On what ground does this battle take place? Ye heart or ye mind? I have given my all, and in return you played the fiddle on my efforts and now expect me to stand in combat with you. Thou shall not assume I don't, for I know you care. You just care for thyself-more. Why shall I fight? Why should I care? Why shall I give you the luxury of my heart when you have already proven you're not man enough to protect it? Why should I make you happy when you did everything to hurt me? Is this guilt you bring before me? Why should I believe you now know what it is I'm worth?

Jamie
And with her sword swinging at its highest and the sun setting in the north, signs of her slowing down are nowhere to be found; is this truly what you want?

Alice
Don't insult me with a question as an answer.

Jamie
Not my intention, my love. I only come in peace. I traveled a long way and have no deceit in my heart, only gifts. For defeat only greets me because you decide to show this nonchalant demeanor, like you don't love me. Fight because every night I cover your thoughts like the stars cover the sky. Fight because neither you nor I believe in giving up on what many die searching for.

Because we believe in fixing what's broken and not running at the first sign of trouble. This is not about one single soul, so to say this is to make me happy and that my moves are out of guilt is blasphemy. You're worth more than the unsolved mysteries of the galaxy. All I want is to be happy. To awake and lie down with a smile on my face. To grow old and live for what God has created us for, love.

Alice
It's impossible to catch the wind in your hand yet you try.

Jamie
I try because no matter where I turn my thoughts to, you're right there. Meet me on the battlefield and let's settle this like adults. Let's engage in battle for love. Let's battle for love.

The Night I Fell in Love with a Nineteen-Year-Old

September 3, 2012
Age: 31

A year ago, from today was our first date. I remember it like it yesterday because we were supposed to go out the week before but had to reschedule because of hurricane Irene. We were supposed to go see Tommy Davidson that night. I was taught never to ask a woman her age, and judging from our conversations via text, there really wasn't a reason to. We met on Facebook. She sent a friend request, I confirmed, and it began. We picked up on each other's humor instantly, without even being around each other. We were finishing each other's sentences before we knew what our favorite colors were. We just clicked. Without trying and without forcing it, we just clicked. There was no way this woman I was talking to was only nineteen.

Then I saw it as she crossed the street. Her smile lit up the sky, and I could see the innocence of a young girl on her face—the look of a pure unbeaten soul. She had never suffered from a broken heart and did not carry around emotional baggage from tainted men who ruin woman's lives. She didn't have that beat up by life and run-down by cheating men look. She looked just like an angel. Unblemished, untouched, gullible, and vulnerable. I knew she was young, but I didn't know how young, until then.

Caroline's Comedy Club is where we met for our first date. It was a beautiful late summer day, and here was the reason why crossing the street now. That peach dress slightly above the knee, those six-inch shoes, and that smile. Oh, what a smile.

I melted as her first words to me in person were, "What's up, shorty?" as we embraced. We were the same size, but that's the humor that I'd grown to love in the last six and a half weeks.

I happened to be standing outside with the host who was young himself, eighteen, I believe, who made small talk by his admiration of my wristwatch as I waited for her to arrive. All he could say as she approached was, "You are a very lucky man."

"I hope so."

She was physically flawless, and I mean straight breathtaking. I couldn't be this lucky, I said to myself.

As we sat for dinner, I quickly excused myself to go to the bathroom. I didn't have to use it; I just needed some time to gather myself because I was in awe. I just stood in front of the mirror and began talking to myself. "Wow, she's beautiful, and young too. I hope she doesn't start giggling on me. Just don't judge, you got this." I took a deep breath and walked back out there.

As we looked at our menus, all I could think about was a scene in Eddie Murphy's stand-up comedy special *Raw* when the lady he was out with just ordered a salad and water. I was hoping she didn't just order a salad and water, and she didn't. That was a relief. We talked and laughed, finally matching gestures to our humor. Her poise and elegance captured me the most. She didn't show a sign of immaturity at all, so she can't be that young. At least, that's what I thought. After dinner, they called our number to be seated for the show. Tonight's headliner was Donnell Rawlings, also known as Ashy Larry from *Chappelle's Show*. There wasn't a cover charge to get in, just a required two-drink minimum.

The waitress came up and asked us what we'd be drinking. I ordered a Jack Daniels on the rocks, and she asked for my identification. "Miss, your ID please." This is when I found out she wasn't old enough to drink. Oh God, I'm at least ten years older than her. I was slightly embarrassed because I knew the waitress knew the actual age gap. So, I asked her, "How old are you?"

"Oh, I'm nineteen."

At that very moment, I just realized that for the last six and a half weeks that I had been conversing with a nineteen-year-old. Wow!

I had practically made my mind up that I wasn't going to move forward after that. It was just too much of an age gap. We couldn't even go out for drinks together. We were from two different eras. I was Carhart Jeans and Polo knitted sweaters, and she was skinny jeans and big sneakers. I was Nas and she was Drake. This was not going to work, but I didn't allow those thoughts to carry on and ruin my night. I moved them to the side and just enjoyed the show. After gut-wrenching laughter and a great performance by Donnell, we walked eight blocks down to Time Square. This is where it began. All eyes were on us. We did look extremely good together that night. And thank the Lord for my boyish looks at thirty because the perception of it didn't reveal the reality of it—that I was ten years older than her.

Out of nowhere, this guy stopped in front of us and begged to take our picture. He offered us a discount. He said he wanted to use our beauty for his display. He directed each shot well, until the last one. He didn't know this was our first date when he asked.

Our First Awkward Moment

He asked us to kiss so he can capture our love; that's verbatim. We both paused for a second and chuckled as we looked at each other because it caught us off guard. My raised eyebrows indicated that it was up to her.

"Okay, I guess," she said.

We stood there, looked at each for a moment as we smiled, and leaned in for the kiss. It was straight out of a movie as our lips touched, giving the photographer exactly what he asked for. No tongue action, just locked lips. People walking by stopped and stared as we stood in the street looking like we were movie stars. The bright lights, moving cars, and crowded sidewalks created a bigger-than-life vibe. We felt like celebrities.

I started to wonder if they were staring because they noticed the age difference, until one lady said, "You two are the prettiest couple I've ever seen."

"Thank you." We smiled.

I paid the photographer, and he handed us our photos. We both walked off caught up in a moment neither one of us had been totally prepared for, but it felt good. I couldn't keep my eyes off her. She was so breathtaking.

I didn't have time to think about how young she was at that time because it didn't crowd my thoughts. Then the next minute I knew, we were thirty blocks up on 72nd street and Broadway. What made me realize that we had walked thirty blocks was because I delivered milk in the area. I was more surprised that she had done it in those heels, impressive I gestured.

We found a little benched area in front of a building that looked like a setting from an old romantic flick.

So, we sat and talked. It was beautiful, but this time we were much closer. I couldn't help myself; I stole a kiss. I'd never felt that much passion. We pulled away after minutes of kissing both in awe.

"Wow," she said.

"Ah man, where did you learn how to kiss like that?" She smiled. "You're a great kisser. How old are you again?"

This was the first time my age had come up. I don't have a clue why this topic was not at the top of our list, but it wasn't.

I replied, "I'm old. What's the oldest ... what's your cutoff age?"

"No more than twenty-five. Anything over that is nasty." I laughed because she was in for a rude awakening, but there it was. After all those conversations via text, after a beautiful dinner, pictures, a walk where we had talked about love and relationships, hopes, dreams, and desires, and probably the best kiss I ever had, we were just finding out how old we were.

"I'm thirty years old. I'll be thirty-one in November," I said. "Wow! I must see your ID. I have to see this."

I gave her my ID, and she couldn't believe it. "You look no more than twenty-one years old. I'm sorry. Wow, I don't know what to say," she said.

"So, how nasty does it feel now?"

"Not nasty at all, actually. Wow."

"Tell me about it. I'm still stuck on the fact that you're nineteen. That's way too young. I don't know."

Right after that last word left my mouth; she leaned over to me again and kissed me. It was just the greatest kiss ever. We sat there in silence as she rested her head on my shoulder.

All I could think about were the negatives. All I could think about was a girl I had dated years back who had been seven years younger than me. The whole time we dated, I had felt more like her father than her man. A friend of mine thought she was a younger sister. I was embarrassed to go out with her. What made it bad was that she didn't have a mind of her own. I had to think for her. On top of that, she had daddy issues. Both of her parents were drug addicts, and she had been raised by the streets.

With no diploma, no Social Security card, and no birth certificate, I had moved her into my place and given her a life. I practically raised her. I got her everything she needed, but she became my shadow instead of her own person. She had no identity of her own. She catered to my dreams and aspirations instead of trying to find her own way in the world. It wasn't her fault though. I did love her. I loved her enough to break up with her before it was too late. I had to send her into the world to discover who she was. I vowed at that moment that I would never date anyone younger than me again.

At that moment in my life, as that nineteen-year- old rested her head on my shoulder, I knew I couldn't do it again. I didn't have time to be raising anybody. I needed a woman. How much of her identity did she have? How much of me would start to show in her?

How would it affect me when she started to talk like me and adopted my habits? Would I be turned off? Because one thing I did know is that she would, at some point, if we made it that far, start to become like me. She was still growing and hadn't come into herself yet. She was only nineteen. There was a great chance that she might eventually grow apart from me. So even though I had just experienced the greatest kiss ever, despite all the compliments from onlookers, I couldn't do it. It would never work.

It was not just that either. She was too innocent, and I was known to break hearts and ruin lives. I couldn't hurt that smile. The chances of her falling head over heels for me was very likely. The chances of my cheating on her and not giving her what a woman deserved was most likely too. I was done with breaking hearts. I didn't want to mess it up for her soul mate. I didn't want to be the one that created those annoying insecurities all men hate. I didn't want to ruin her, and most likely, I would.

As I sighed, an old man came out the building, dragging his feet as he turned, and he stood right in front of us. He stared for a few seconds and then he said, "Many died searching for what I see in the two of you. And as beautiful as the two of you are, I'm going to have to ask you to excuse me so I can sit."

We got up from the bench and thanked him. I had never been asked to move by a compliment before. As we walked off, he shouted out, "Do what needs to be done to stay together!" We just turned around and smiled as we walked back downtown. This time, holding hands.

What a crazy night. In just one night our lives had been forged together as one by a stranger. In just one night, a love not even created yet was assumed.

All I kept thinking about was what kind of energy we must have been giving off. If that energy was being read by others, then maybe giving this a shot wouldn't be a bad idea. At that moment, I decided to give love a try. I was scared. I didn't know if I was ready yet.

If I wasn't ready, could I be honest with her and let her go instead of leading her on like I've done in my past? Could I be a better, unselfish man and not use my experience to manipulate her? Could I be real? Could she give me what I needed instead of what she thought I wanted? Could she not wear her feelings on her shoulders and keep the chase alive? Could she find the right words to say to put me in my place despite her age and inexperience? Would she be weak and allow me to run all over her? Would she understand the things I needed to sacrifice to accomplish my goals? Did she know how to support me? If I was down and out and needed help would I have to ask, or would she know and offer?

Would she rub my back after a long day of work? Would I come home to a clean house and food on the table? Would she love my daughter like her very own? Would she know what she wants or expect me to know it for her? Could I actually fall in love with a nineteen-year-old and really expect all of these things?

As we walked back downtown, we talked about how much we had enjoyed ourselves.

Then she asked me, "So, if I'm way too young, and you are way too old, what do we do now? My inexperience and what you may expect might clash."

I just shook my head and said, "Wow, I like that. That was on point."

It was that very statement that revealed a great deal of possibility, even though she may have been right, I'm just glad I stuck around to find out.

"Well, I guess we just follow this feeling and see where it takes us."

"How do you know this feeling I have I like?"

"Because you haven't stopped smiling. Plus, you're blushing. Now unless your cheeks are frozen, I'm pretty sure it's the very feeling I have."

"And what feeling is that?"

"That despite our age difference and preferences, there has to be a reason why this feels so good. Plus, I like adventures, and I think it would be one to find out what everyone seems to see in us."

"You and your smooth-talking self. Always know the right thing to say, huh?"

"It's much, much easier when it's associated with the right feeling."

She called me an old head as we both laughed and walked down the stairs to the A train at the 59th Street station. I never told her, but that was the night I fell in love with a nineteen-year- old.

"If you give a person too much too soon, they will fall in love with your hand and not your heart."

A Conversation with a Friend about Love
April 11, 2009
Age: 28

Anonymous
My greatest pain right now is being in love with someone I
cannot have. So, my question is, is it necessary to be with
the person you believe is your soul-mate? Or can you
live with knowing that person already has someone else,
but deep down inside, he feels the same way you feel?

Jamai
It's not up to you. What you believe has nothing to do
with what it really is. What you believe may be stimulated
by lust as well. You could be lying to yourself. He could be
lying to himself. How do you know what this person
feels, honestly, because even if this person verbalizes it,
how do you know he knows what he truly wants if his
actions don't follow? A lot of times what we want is lust
driven, especially in our youth. And I consider our 20's to
be youth in regard to love.

Anonymous
How can one tell the difference between lust and love? I
think that is the reason I'm in this predicament I am in
now, I don't the difference.

Jamai
Lust is for a moment; love is for a lifetime. Love can't be
measure. It's timeless. It's forever. Lust has an expiration
date. You know its lust if after you have sex, and that
excitement leaves. Or it strictly remains on the physical.
It's an attraction that really doesn't go pass the physical.
Good sex can stretch a bad relationship a long time. A lot of
people fall for lust thinking it's love, then try to trust that
love. Love can never come from lust. But to determine what
it is is quite simple.

For me, my mind must be intellectually befriended. I must have mental orgasms. I must love to talk to you. We must believe in mostly the same things. I have to admire what you're about. I must love your lifestyle and sense of humor. All these things must come before sex is involved. It makes the physical connection that much better when you connect with the mind first. You could be with someone for years, and in those years, it was lust that kept you together. Which is why you must ask yourself, is it real or did you convince yourself? Is it love or an addictive clinging? Addictive clinging is the tree from the seed of lust.

Anonymous
Addictive clinging?

Jamai
I can't remember if I read that somewhere or not, but it's when you have been around a person for so long you cling to them. Being around them becomes addictive. You become an addict for their presence. You become **dependent** on it. Love is not keeping you there, it's the fear of being by yourself. You've become so used to the system the two of you created, your fear of separation convinces you to believe it's love. This is a whole other subject, but yeah, its' pretty deep what people call love when their really in lust.

Anonymous
Thanks for the enlightenment. Now inspire me.

Jamai
Just take it one day at a time. Your knight in shining armor is out there. He will find you if you continue to be you and never compromise your standards. Know what you want from a man, and if he is not what you want him to be, don't waste your time. When you do eventually find love, it will be unexpected, it will be different. This person will

116   RANDOM THOUGHTS

give you a mental orgasm without trying. It will be in a place you would have not dreamed of in many moons. Just be you and follow your dreams. Be authentic. Live to find yourself first and embrace your life's mission. Love finds you when you first love yourself. So, my advice to you is to focus on what makes your heart dance and makes your soul smile. When you accomplish this, he will come. Just let love for self be what emanates from you. This will create a powerful aura of attraction and love will find you.

Some Would Say

June 7, 2010
Age: 29

Some would say that I am an intellectual bully. Some would say I use my intellect to deprecate the feeble-minded to shadow my own insecurities. Some would say my ego outshines my intelligence. Some would say I enlighten them. Some would say thank you. And then some would want to say thank you, but their pride would cod block that hugely humble attribute. Some would say he's too cocky and self-centered. Some would say if you knew of his past you would understand his present. Some would say he's arrogant. Some would say it's not what he says; it's how he says it, and mainly how you take it. Some would say that he's an asshole. Some would say he just speaks his mind with no regard for how you would feel about it. Just don't be so sensitive. We all know that the truth hurts, and nobody wants to hear it, some would say. Some would say he's just being a Sagittarius.

He's just being Jamai. Some would say you just don't get him. Some would say if you don't understand him then you weren't meant to know him. Some would say he's great. But then some would say, yeah, but his failures outshine his accomplishments. Damn, a mind would be a terrible thing to waste, some would say. Some would say he's dripping in potential. Some would say I'll believe it when I see it. Some would say he's too much on himself. Some would say he thinks he's God's gift to women and a blessing to anyone who crosses his path. Some would say only time will tell. That's what some would say. But to be honest with you, I don't care what some would say or how some would take it. Because when it's all said and done, all I care about is what the sum would say when I go to the bank. Always be, you.

RANDOM THOUGHTS

I'm Just Me

April 27, 2008
Age: 27

It is known that wise men are wise before not after,
and that smart men learn from their mistakes.
So, the question I ask myself is,
if in one day you'll learn just by being you and making
mistakes,

why must I play back seat and be passive throwing clouds in
front of my Sun for the non-gifted sake of the insecure, when
I made the mistakes that made me great. This would be like
taking the soul from Michael Jackson's feet,

or a pen from Maya Angelou's hand so she couldn't
weave. I dare men content with little say I can't be me for
the sake of their own fears and insecurities. I know my
presence alone makes you realize what you're missing.

And that I embody the virtues of character, confidence, self-
knowledge and wisdom. But it's not my fault your
intelligence is not near I, and that there's no way you can
articulate quite like I, you are not prepared and that's felt
more than what one can see with the eye, insulting myself
by entertaining what does not apply, I will not comply.

That would be emotions superseding intelligence of what's
inconsequential to growth and development. Jesus spoke the
truth; they threw rocks and stones. I speak the truth with
no rocks or stones and because I don't shine my truth
remains unknown. When the truth is you lack what I know,
instead of using me your pride stagnates your growth.

I was told to compromise my intelligence and speak to be understood, but why can't they compromise their ignorance and look up what wasn't understood?

Instead of laughing at me, ask me, and I gladly tell you the meaning. That pride you have is exactly why we're not going anywhere as a people.

And who you deal with is nothing but a reflection, of your moral standards and conceptions, showing the consequences of misdirection. Anytime anything intellectually stimulating passes you by you never catch the interception.

Yes, your rhetoric is convincing, but you're a pretender who lacks the discipline to be a contender. You're mad at me because I am and you're stuck at potential, I'm twenty-seven years old with ancient Asian old man wisdom.

I know it hurts your soul to see me stand tall while you're crippled. Opportunity knocked and they went past your window. Left the key under the floor mat and you still climbed through the window. It hurts to observe the insecurities of an unstable ego, but we know.

Look, you can call me what you want to; I don't care if this didn't pinch and you don't feel me. I don't care if this reflects arrogance and you run from my literature like nosebleeds. I don't care if you call me a cocky, self-centered condescending bastard who thinks he's better than me because other than me is who I refuse to be. So love me or hate me but you will respect me.

Thinking highly of yourself

vs

Thinking you are better than others

There's a difference.

RANDOM THOUGHTS

Be aware of who you associate with. If your circle is comprised of close-minded, unmotivated friends who live in poverty consciousness, then you will be brought down. Instead, seek to manifest a group of positive, goal-oriented friends who live in abundance consciousness. This will help push you ahead in life.

And remember, understanding is more valuable then information. Someone can know you, but don't understand you at the same time. And if people don't understand you, it's okay. Then that means they weren't meant to know you.

Also, anything you say after 'I am' you become. Words cast powerful spells. That's why it called 'spelling'. Choose your words wisely.

Like, if you say, "Life is short' or 'I'm getting old', your body will prematurely age. This is because the cells in your body react to everything that your mind says. Be aware of what thoughts are being affirmed in your mind. Because once you believe it, it manifests it in form.

Without Him

Journal Entry
January 1, 2013
Age: 32

For seven whole years of my life, I've lived across the street from my biological father, and I never knew. When I moved to Queens when I was eight years old, I remember sitting at the dinner table and asking my mother why I looked so different from my brother and sister, my having a darker complexion. A few days later, they walked with me to my school park and explained that the man I've been calling daddy all my known life was not actually the man who brought me into this world.

It didn't stop me from calling him daddy, of course. Five years later, about a year after the death of the man I have known as my father, my aunt took me to meet my biological father. I remember being amazed by the fact that he lived directly across the street in the neighboring project buildings I grew up in. I didn't start asking questions why, until a few years ago. Why doesn't a man who knows his son is but a few steps away reach out? My father, the man who raised me until his death, was a very intimidating man, but I don't see his not allowing my biological father to be a man.

I still don't know the whole story behind it and will never know, but I'm content with that. For years, after many questions, I realized he just didn't care. The most my biological father ever did for me was sign over his rights so I could receive money from the man who raised me when he passed away. As I got older, I stopped blaming him and put the blame on my mother. Her being miss independent and all, she probably wanted nothing to do with him.

She always said he never stepped up to the plate. I always thought maybe she didn't allow him to, but that was just my anger toward her. She just didn't force him to, and in my opinion, she shouldn't have had to.

I put the past behind me and tried to build a relationship with him anyway because there was no reason to hold a grudge. I decided to reach out to him instead, to at least have a future. But every time I got around him, I just wanted to ask him what happened. What was the story? He never took the initiative to tell me, so I concluded that it was exactly what it was: he just didn't care. I convinced myself to leave the questions alone, leave the whys alone, and just live for today. I mean, he is my father.

As time went by, I really started to see what he was about, and I became scared for myself. Here was a fifty-five-year-old man still living in the same room he grew up in as a child. A fifty-five-year-old man still living with his mother. All I kept saying to myself was that I had loser genes swimming around in my gene pool, and I would not be like him no matter how similar our situations were. (Meaning the situation of living at home with mommy.)

I moved to Washington Heights in September of 2011, which is not that far from him. As I was not that far from him, I began hanging out with him more. The more I hung around, the more I saw where I got my sense of humor and personality from. I started to see where his morals, values and principles laid also. Then it hit me; if he's this way now, he was probably worse at the time of my birth. This man has no principles. He's like a big kid, no values, nothing. What could he have possibly taught me? That was the moment when I realized that every man is not meant to raise a child, even though they can produce them. Just because a man can make a kid, doesn't mean he has what is necessary to raise it.

For years, I just couldn't fathom how you know something you created exists and not make your presence known. I realized that all those years of asking why this and why that was for nothing. I now have a clarifying displeasure of realizing I would have most likely been worse off with him in my life.

So, I thank you, Mr. Jackson, honestly. I'm not mad at you at all. I appreciate you not caring. I would have rather you not been there at all than have a half of a father playing with my emotions. I just hope, I don't have in me, what you have in you, for what you did to me, what I don't want to do to my own kids.

My Journey Up North: Bronchoscopy

April 19, 2007
Age: 26

The results from my saliva test came back from the lab today and determined that whatever issue I am having with my lungs is not due to TB, ruling that and cancer out. But it's some type of fungus. Fortunately, all that is required is to see a pulmonary specialist to get a biopsy done. That's where they stick a tube through my nostril and down my throat to recover the bacteria from my lungs. Once that is done, I will be given a pill of some sort to clear it up.

That Morning

It's 4:00 am. Night still covers the land that hides in the dark as I prepare myself to go out on a medical leave. While getting ID'd by the sergeant to make sure I am who I'm supposed to be, we immediately get into a verbal altercation. One of the transporters quickly assumes my attitude was of anger and a lack of respect for authority and labels me a problem, not that maybe I didn't like his talking to me like I was five years old. It's always an egotistical prick with power issues that feels the need to be disrespectful, to speak the obvious. Respect is given, not earned. My present circumstances do not make me less of a man.

"Show some respect. He's the boss," said the transporter. "No, he's your boss. To me, he's just another man who thinks labeling himself a French-Canadian takes away from the fact that he's black."

"Listen, get rid of your attitude because you have no wins," said the transporter.

"You're absolutely right." And that was the last thing I said.

We get inside the unit and pull off into the dark hours of the morning. I'm unexpectedly reminded of a very creepy scene in a very bad psycho-thriller. Two big white men sit quietly in the front cab listening to country music, doing their jobs, and showing no emotion on their faces, with firearms and toothpicks.

When we finally make it to the hospital, the shuffle of my chained feet draws a lot of eyes. But I am used to this kind of attention, so it didn't bother me. After speaking with the doctor, I find out that I'm not getting a CAT scan but a bronchoscopy, which is more direct look at the lungs. As she goes over the purpose of the procedure, she brings up the worst-case scenario. They could accidentally poke a hole in my lungs and have the air leak out, resulting in the collapse of my lungs (death). She says that rarely happens, but still, I don't like how that rarely fell out her mouth.

After they numb the inside of my left nostril and place sensors on my chest that will monitor my heart rate, I was out. I woke up, and it felt like only five minutes have passed. Brushing's were obtained for analysis, so I must wait until the cultures come back to find out what's next. Until then, I just hope it doesn't grow into anything more serious.

The Incarceration of a Correction Officer

July 17, 2007
Age: 26

He's my secretary. He takes my calls for me. He tells me when I have a delivery (package). Like a doorman, he informs me of any visits. When my doctors want to see me, they set up an appointment through him. Like an assistant, he makes sure I'm never late for anything. I tell him something is wrong with my toilet, and he takes care of it. He takes me shopping for my food and toiletries. He lets me know when my breakfast, lunch, and dinner is ready. He even brings my mail. And if he really cares, he protects me from other inmates and stands up for me. And when I have somewhere to go off the grounds, he drives me there and back. If I'm lucky, he may even buy me McDonald's.

Most of them work sixteen hours. They sleep here, eat what we eat, walk the yard, and get paid to be here. We answer to them, *they* answer to the white shirts. Some do twenty, twenty-five, and even thirty years in jail. They know all the slang, and some talk it. Some are even around us more than they're around their own families.

Like inmates, some COs have more power and pull than others. Some even act like inmates and are worse off mentally. They even bring drugs to inmates. They bring the lifestyle that got them put in prison back to them. Sometimes it's hard to tell who's who. Some COs will get you hurt by other inmates. Some COs will get you hurt by other COs. Everybody has a clique, a gang. There's really no difference mentally between an inmate and an officer, for some of them.

Jail is a different world than the outside world. But both inmate and correction officer is mentally locked-up. The money and benefits will never compensate for what this job does to their souls. We are not their greatest worry; they are. They lie, snitch, and set each other up, just like we do. A CO is not an inmate's greatest worry; we are. In both worlds, there are those who hate and those who are jealous and want what you have or want to be where you are. I wouldn't wish their life or job on anyone. It's a job where you get paid to be incarcerated. It's a place where you adapt to your surroundings, unconsciously and inadvertently.

He sits and reads to pass time, occupying his mind as he ganders at the clock, wanting the same thing I want when I look at the calendar, to go home, to be free.

"It sucks, doesn't it," I ask. He replies,
"What sucks?"

"Being locked up."

He smirks and says, "You're funny."

But deep down he knows there's truth in what I said as his smirk fades back to black. He has one comfort over me, and it's not that he knows when he is going home, when he will be released, because I know when I will as well. What he has over me is that his time is done by the hour. And my time is done one day at a time. And when you think about it, looking at the clock every hour might not be that comforting in the moment.

Incarcerated means to be subjected to confinement. To be confined is to hold down, to keep within limits, to close in. Even though they get to leave and go home, they will always be incarcerated.

Religious Loopholes Concerning Same-Sex Marriage and Homosexuality

May 21, 2012
Age: 31

> *The problem with religion is that it has man*
> *believing he has all the answers when he doesn't.*
>
> *— Bill Maher*

Religious leaders in both the white and black communities do not believe in same-sex marriage; they believe in the union of man and woman as the Bible says. So, being that that understanding is understood, there's no reason to reference back because we know where they stand and why. You say you're not for sure whether a man's attraction to another man or a woman to woman is from preference or orientation. You say you understand that the X and Y chromosomes factor to a certain degree and that every man is born with a certain amount of femininity in him and every woman some masculinity. You say you also know couples whose small boys started showing signs of homosexuality as early as five. (Even though their sexuality hasn't been explored yet, research says most young boys express their sexuality with other boys first as preteens.)

No gay gene has been found, so to say that people are born that way would be barking up a tree where the roots have not yet been found. But what has been discovered and realized is that most gay men have more homosexual relatives on their mother's side of the family than their fathers. Why that is can only lead to rhetoric of unproven facts and speculation.

And remember, homosexuality is a normal occurrence is the animal kingdom. Yes, there are gay and lesbian animals too. You do have an argument with the preference or orientation point because studies have shown that over time the reclaiming, if it ever was claimed, of one's heterosexual identity (re)surfaces, but mainly in women and a very small percentage in men. So, if one can flip back and forth, is it a psychological problem, and does it have a beginning, as all things do? Is it anger or fear? Could it be that some of these females have been raped and turned off by men, hurt, battered and abused by men, both lovers and fathers? Are these men confused, experimenting, or weak? Do they care or does it matter? Nonetheless, it seems that being gay or straight for some is a choice. I've learned that speculation on this topic is endless, and I'm pretty sure many gay men would argue that it's not a choice for them. I just never understood how some lesbian woman who do not like men have relations with women who look like men.

And like you and me, they have wants and needs as humans as well. So, if they breathe, bleed, and sweat like you and me, and love like you and me, why does their sexual preference make them different than you and me, assuming you're straight of course?

If a man or woman isn't intentionally going against God's word, and the Bible states that every man is created equal and should be treated justly, doesn't going against same-sex marriage make you a hypocrite? And please don't say it's what you believe in because you're only contradicting yourself. And that's the thing about religion. Facts can be smacking you dead in the face, but in contradiction people still hold on to what they believe in. Why? Well that's another topic I'm pretty sure I touched on somewhere in this book.

Religion goes hand in hand with ignorance. I can throw facts and numbers that prove otherwise, but because a book says something to the contrary you ignore it. There's nothing stronger than belief, especially in religion. Even if the facts are stacked against you, a man will stand in ignorance for what he believes is truth. A person is smart, but people are stupid. All men are created equal, your Bible says, but because your Bible also states that marriage is the union between man and woman, it's not your fault you're a hypocrite or confused. Your source is as well. This is just my opinion.

Koala Bear Sun

The Journey to Reach Spiritual Enlightenment, Part 2

"Straight from the slums of the Shaolin Temple of Zen Zen Zah, please give a warm spiritual embrace to, Koala Bear Sun of Higher Consciousness beyond the Mind and Thought of Self for Holistic Salvation."

The audience claps enthusiastically.

"Thank you. Thank you."

"That's a very long name," says Pope-ra

"I know. It was conceived after the realization that my birth name does not express, in my opinion, who I am in my totality and what I've achieved and plan on achieving."

"Okay, well, welcome to the Pope-ra In-heat show. I'm Pope-ra, and I'm in heat."

"Our guest today is on a quest for spiritual enlightenment to stretch and strengthen his being in hopes of becoming immortal. So, what made you choose this particular journey and how were you inspired?"

"We all know it's not intellectually fashionable, Pope-Rah, to try to achieve immortality when society believes there's a God in the sky. Which is nothing but a projection of the human mind trying to find the purpose for his being, which is actually the ego in search of his biological thought."

"The brain, or the power pellet of untapped functionality that I call it, only has a usage of 6 percent. So, it has 94 percent of unused energy. This unused power is what inspires me."

"So, what if I could build a helmet under the teachings of Xavier that could unlock this untapped brain power by manipulating the purpose of the brain chemicals that help cells communicate with one another, giving more power to the cerebral cortex. Thus, activating this 94 percent. Imagine that."

"My fourth master, Master Oda, who came to this planet in search of the Hair Club for Extraterrestrials with Extraordinary Intellectual Power, also known as the Temple of Supreme Dome. Which is nothing but a big head full of hair that recedes every few seconds to advertise its business of rejuvenating the hair particles of alien life- forms, which was built upon the ruins of Castle Grayskull after He-Man couldn't pay his back taxes and She-Ra took half, has used the force to access or tap into this unused portion of the brain. His concubine, Obi-Two Shonobi, who knew Master Splinter before he was a rat, also has the force."

"My kid brother, Booger Buddha, who is a snot-nosed genius with the power to move objects with his mind, doesn't even walk anymore. He has tapped into this power. He's a gliding douchebag with a remarkable power to attract. He's a master of the Law of Attraction and just recently hit the lotto for $100 million. Imagine a big-headed baby who glides across the floor while peeing on himself. He doesn't talk either. But somehow is able to communicate using the force. Here he is in an interview after he hit the lotto."

"So, Booger, the numbers, how did you pick the numbers?" says the reporter.

"That's a stupid question; next."

"Okay, what do you think about luck being a big factor in this picture?"

"Are you insulting my intelligence, lady? Negative, I attracted this. See, your energy sends out a frequency to the universe and vibrates whatever your thoughts may be dwelling on and brings it back to you. Which takes heavy meditation and grounding to do. In this case, I have about another year or two in diapers and with the other physical needs of a toddler, which my genius can't seem to shed, so I decided to hit the lotto."

"But aren't you too young to receive the winnings?" says the reporter.

"Technically, yes. That's why I have parents, stupid. Do you think I would go down there myself? You are what you think, whether you're conscious or unconscious of those thoughts. Your aura can do more for you than your conversation, and right now this interview is over, I don't like your energy."

"One last question please, I hear your brother, Koala Bear Sun, is building a helmet that will allow him to tap into the 94 percent of unused brainpower."

"Yeah, well, he's an impatient and misguided fool. He is extremely jealous of me because I'm a Master at 2 years old. So, we don't talk. He's a psycho," says Booger Buddha.

Pope-ra In heat asks Koala Bear Sun of Higher Consciousness beyond the Mind and Thought of Self for Holistic Salvation, "So, your brother says you're jealous of him and that you two haven't talked for a while, is it true?"

"I wouldn't say I'm jealous Pope-ra. He just has his thing going for him, he has found his calling and I'm still searching, so yeah, it can be frustrating watching a 2-year-old walk in his purpose. And now that he's rich, it hurts even more. It's like a slap in the face you know.

"But when I'm done building my helmet, my newfound level of consciousness will heighten my creativity, allowing me to invent a product that will revolutionize how we bottle water."

"Oh really", says Pope-ra.

"Yes, it's called Powdered-Water, and it comes in packages like Kool-Aid. Yes, water in a powder form. Simply add water and poof! The powdery substance turns into water that can become any desired amount. I know, I know, genius. But this is just an example of what I'm achieving on my journey of spiritual enlightenment thus far. I am one with myself, and myself is one with the wind." (Hmmmmmm, may the force be with you.)

To Be Continued...

OF A PHILOSOPHY MAJOR DROPOUT

"Above all, don't lie to yourself. The man who lies to himself and listens to his own lie comes to a point that he cannot distinguish the truth within him, or around him, and so loses all respect for himself and for others. And having no respect he ceases to love." - Fyodor Dostoyevsky.

"The greater the artist, the greater the doubt. Perfect confidence is granted to the less talented as a consolation prize." - Robert Hughes

RANDOM THOUGHTS

My Journey Up North: Medical Update

December 17, 2007
Age: 27

I dropped a slip to see a doctor because it's been 2 months and I still hadn't heard anything about my lungs. The bronchoscopy showed that I had two abscesses in the lower right region of my right lung. They gave me some antibiotics to take, but after my visit to the hospital in October it showed that the antibiotics hadn't worked, and the abscess was still there. After I explained to the doctor what I was told about possible surgery, he dug a little deeper into the history and concluded that it needed to be taken care of ASAP. He told me that pulmonary department would have me waiting around for two years and that it was a good thing I had checked in on the matter. He scheduled me to see a surgeon for consultation purposes to discuss the procedure, and I would have an operation for the removal of the abscess before I went home.

Two days after my birthday, I was called out to the hospital in Syracuse for a consult. It was November 29, 2007, a dark, gloomy, and cold morning, but the relief of finally moving forward with the procedure filled my being. I walked through the hospital chained at the feet and hands as I entered a room with one officer while the other stood guard. It looked like I was in for war crimes against the United States.

Then she walked in, Dr. Dexter, five foot two, Chinese, and so cute. I felt comfortable with her as my surgeon. She explained the surgery, from cutting under my shoulder blade, to taking a rib out, to cutting the bottom part of my right lung off. I was scared but didn't show it.

She then went on to say how I would be given a epidural for the pain and that they would hold me in the hospital for five to seven days after the surgery. In due time, I would be able to do everything I was doing now, mainly because I was young and healthy and exercised a lot. On Friday, December 14 they took some blood from me. I was told not to take any aspirin or medication for seven days, which indirectly told me that the surgery was on the twenty- first of the month. I was having lung surgery.

Unconscious Knowledge

November 24, 2009
Age: 28

It's not having knowledge that makes you smart;
it's the application of it that determines your intelligence.
—Author Unknown

A question that I have asked myself time and time again is, am I as smart as I think I am? I've observed, experienced, and obtained a lot of knowledge in my twenty-eight years of life, and sometimes I feel like I don't remember anything. And that's because I can't articulate to you, like I would like to about something profound from off the top of my head. Sometimes, I feel like I pushed information out of my head by putting more in it.

Then a situation arose where I was asked for my opinion; now what shocked me was that I was able to supply this individual with more than just your regular everyday advice. I was really able to, with great confidence, speak about this particular topic almost as if I was an expert, or at least that's how he felt. I didn't know I knew these things until I was asked. Here I thought I was just wasting my time, stuffing myself with knowledge that I thought I had forgotten, and I knew something; the benefits had finally appeared. And this is what I call, *unconscious knowledge*: not being conscious of the wealth of knowledge you have until a situation presents itself.

But what if the situation doesn't present itself because you isolate yourself from the world, and your true potential and ability doesn't get a chance to breathe? That's why you must put yourself out there in the world where there's a constant flow of situations.

Surround yourself in an atmosphere that compliments your mind so what you know can present itself. Attend events, seminars, and things that will bring you in contact with people. It would be a crime not to give the world your education, experience and your ideas. Let this motivate you and give you the confidence to throw yourself out in the wind to be guided by the hands of your untold knowledge. The only thing stopping you is what you think you don't know. The structural learning the educational system has set up in this country is unreliable. You are needed. Trust in yourself and your abilities, and I guarantee you will amaze yourself every time.

The great difficulty in education is to get experience out of ideas.
– George Santayana

*What's the sense of knowing when your
education is not cultivated through practice?*

– Jamai Wray

Acceptance Speech

December, 7, 2011
Age: 30 years old

First and foremost, I would like to thank the Universe for condensing its energy in the form of matter to create my life. Its great to be conscious of myself. Secondly, and most importantly, I would like to thank myself for all the decisions I made both bad and good, which put me on the path that got me here. I want to thank my mother for kicking me out of the house all those times. Thank you for putting me in group homes and for choosing your husband over me.

I also want to thank her for all the times she said I was pipe dreaming, how stupid I was and how she should have flushed me down the toilet. And that I will be just like my loser father, I really do appreciate that. It's that experience that made me fearless, made me adaptable, made me not allow anyone to get close to me and to not trust anyone. It really helped construct the much-needed amount of selfishness, to stay focus on myself and my dreams. I have great power to produce because I lived for a very long time just to prove you wrong. Without that anger and rage to prove you wrong I don't know where I would have gotten the motivation. So, thank you.

I would also like to thank Waynisha for cheating on me while I was incarcerated in Connecticut. It's because of you I wrote my first song. Which led to this book and my versatility to pretty much write everything. I never got a chance to thank you for that. Thank you. I would like to thank all the Correctional facilities that housed me from New York to Connecticut and Texas. Thank you for giving me the time I didn't know I needed to figure out who I was.

To study my behavior and introspect. I mean, with freedom, I didn't have time to work on me. I was too caught up in the matrix, in the deception and lies of this world working to make someone else rich. I was able to focus on being a better artist, without the worries of food, shelter and clothing, because it was all provided, so thank you for that. It's because of you all I became a man. I want to thank the walls in my cell for listening to me all those nights. I would also like to thank all the C.O.'s in Marcy Correctional Facility for making sure I had books on 'How to write screenplays', 'Scripts made for TV' and just material that helped me become a better writer. I just wanna go back real quick and thank my mother one more time. The first thing I ever stole on the streets, was a hero from the corner store bodega because I was hungry, that first time she kicked me out. I will never forget standing on that corner at 14 looking around trying to figure out where I was going to sleep and what was I going to eat. That right there was the beginning of my doing what I had to do to survive. Which made me a warrior of life. A survivor. Even though it was wrong, and I wouldn't recommend this type of behavior. I wouldn't be able to survive anywhere under any circumstances, if it wasn't for you making that decision, to choose a man over your son, just six months after my father died. I want to thank all my close friends I grew up with for being jealous of me. It was in you guys fear and honesty that made me realize what a friend is. Thank you for not supporting me and I apologize to for expecting you, when you don't even support yourself. So, thank you. The road was tough. I wanted to give up countless times, but I didn't because all of you were on my mind. This isn't about proving to myself I can do it because I already knew I would be standing up here one day. This is about proving to you I was right about me and about life. To all my dreamers out there, remember this, my mother always told me, she'll believe it when she sees it, no, in order to believe it, you must first see it. (points to head). Thank you.

My Journey Up North: Surgery

December 21, 2007
Age: 27

After a four-hour procedure and given other pain medications to soothed the excruciating pain that comes with taking a rib out, I was finally abscess free. Cause: unknown. Assumption: born with it. Smoking over the years maybe triggered what was already there, even though it had been seventy-eight months since I had smoked a cigarette. My mother did smoke the whole time she was pregnant with me, maybe it's from that.

As usual, as fast as I went out, the faster I came too. I woke up to four medical staff staring at me, asking me how I was doing as I noticed I had a tube in my private area and a tube under my right breast. The incision where the surgery took place was actually through my back. The tube in my private area was so I'd be able to go to the bathroom during and after surgery without actually knowing.

Saturday at 4:55 pm, my brother, aunt, nephew, and cousin showed up to my surprise. Being in Syracuse brought me a lot closer to the city, as opposed to being thirty miles from Canada, so the trip wasn't bad at all if they didn't run into any traffic, and it was a straight drive. It would have been the bomb to see my mother and sister too, but they couldn't make it. I hadn't seen them in over a year.

The next morning, I scared everybody. I got out my bed and sat in the chair to prepare for breakfast, and I passed out. I almost fell on my face, but Jessica, my nurse, caught me. The officer who was on guard said it had looked like a mini seizure, and that's what I think it was. cause: unknown.

Later, that day, I was chauffeured in my wheelchair to take an X-ray to see the results. I was able to stand up on my own to take the X-ray. I took a deep breath, exhaled, and then fell again, luckily back in the arms of Jessica.

I was moved upstairs to the medical unit where they housed the inmates. I was told that the X-ray showed air and fluid in my lungs and that the half of my right lung I still had was still deflated. I didn't panic because everybody else showed no emotion or worry, so obviously it wasn't that bad. They stuck a tube in my chest that next morning and drained the fluid out. Tuesday, they took another X-ray and my lungs had inflated and the fluid was gone. I didn't want to leave the hospital. Of course, who wants to go back to jail?

By Wednesday, I was back incarcerated. I was told that in a matter of days I would be able to shower. When I got back to the facility (jail), the nurses examined my wound because they had heard that a new procedure for closing wounds had been used on me. No staples or stitches were used, I was glued back together. I could barely walk, and because it was the middle of winter, I had to wear a mask on my face so the cold air wouldn't reach my lungs. All the weight I had gained, I lost. Everything I did I needed assistance with. Good thing I hadn't made any enemies.

I took four ibuprofens a day for the pain and was told not to stop taking them until told so. Not understanding the severity of my surgery, I thought that because I was no longer feeling any pain that I could cut down on the dose. Boy, was I so wrong. I had never in my life felt a pain so excruciating. I could not move. I was begging the Lord to stop the pain until the two much needed ibuprofens kicked in. The thought of having half my right lung removed never crossed my mind. The cost of the surgery always makes me wonder, if I would had never got locked up, I would had never caught it in time, not only that, but I would had not been able to pay for the surgery as well. Being incarcerated literally saved my life.

Milestone

Journal Entry
January 15, 2013
Age: 32

After fourteen months, I have finally completed what I set out to do. After so many revisions, so many doubts and uncertainties, so many dry moments of writer's block, I can finally move forward into the next stage of this process. I have to head out to the bank really quick though and put some more money into my business account. The initial $1,174.50 for the edit jumped up an extra $23. I just had to get this last piece in here.

This is a great achievement for me, after all the songs I've written and all the money on studio time I've spent, even when I secretly doubted my ability to be the greatest rapper ever. I've never felt so content about a project I've done in my life—a project I completed. Now I can begin my journey, a journey where the main goal is just to be happy in what I'm doing, not doing it just because I have no other choice.

What's the Point?

February 9, 2008
Age: 27
Revised: June 11, 2012

So, what's the point? Why am I here? Why are you there? Why are you reading this? What's the point?

Could it be to hear something helpful, guiding or, inspirational? Do I tickle your fancy? Does my pain give you pleasure? Do you find me funny? Is this you supporting my book? Are you here for clarity, to please your intellectual side, or to impress someone else by acting like you have one? What do you want out of this? What's the point?

Why do you do what you do for a living? Could it be because in what you want to do you lack skill, will, ambition, the balls, drive, purpose, or strength, so you succumb to your fear and settle for what you feel you have no choice to do? What's the point? You talk about change and making your life better. You talk about someday becoming more than what you are. You claim that one day this will not define you, but you do nothing about it. So, what's the point?

Are you doing what you have to do, what you feel you need to do, or what you want to do? Excuse me, I said that one already, so, what's the point? Why do I repeat myself like I'm unaware that I'm going in circles? That's because the truth is that I am aware. I just need to fill up space and add to the word count. That's the point. Why is there so much mystery in questions without answers? Why do you smoke when you know it causes cancer? Why do I say I care and love myself when my actions speak the opposite?

Why do I pretend to be faithful and promise not to break your heart and then go out and cheat and get mad when I get caught? What's the point? Why chase what feels good in the moment when I know there's no future in the moment? Why praise a God I don't know when I can praise somebody I don't know—myself? Are you happy or settling? Are you content or confused? Are you not satisfying the needs of today with the hopes of a promising tomorrow? If so, what's the point if tomorrow is not promise?

My mother called me a fool for dropping out of college. She's mad because I wanted to be a rapper and take over the world. She said a mind is a terrible thing to waste, kicked me out the house, and said some very harsh things. But I did what I did, and she eventually let me back in and now supports everything I do. So, what was the point?

Now I can ask, why are we fighting a perceived losing battle in the Middle East? But what's the point? Why waste time with a question like that when I'm trying to get to the point of this point? Could procrastination serve as a gateway leading us to our point? To procrastinate is to put off intentionally the doing of something that should be done. So, if procrastination is the point of this poem and you're sitting here reading it, I should thank you and at the same time tell you to get off your ass when you're done reading and do what needs to be done to get to your point. Either way, if neither one of us ever gets to the point we're trying to make when we're done, we could just turn to the person sitting next to us or look in the mirror and say, what's the point? What is the freaking point of all this?

Final Thought

*The thought that leads to no action
is not thought – it is dreaming.*
—Author Unknown

In every situation, whether good or bad, there's a defining moment. This moment usually arises when all mental means of comprehension have been exhausted. Whether your current circumstances are of your own or not, there's always a moment of clarity. It usually surfaces when your mind is occupied with something else. You're ah-ha moment. With my being in the post- production phase of the very book you're reading.

Trying to put together the funds to get it edited, I couldn't quite make out what exactly God was trying to say when I received that text from my landlord. What does a moment so random mean? What am I being tested on? Why am I still struggling to be who I know I am? Haven't I gone through enough? Haven't I've been honest and authentic with myself? Haven't I remained true to what I believe in? Haven't I seen enough? Where is the reward for following your dreams?

Everything at that moment didn't **seem to** make sense at all. But I came too far to just give up and no matter how random it was, I had to have the mindset that everything happens for a reason and to keep pushing. When I think back to when I got arrested and the cops **putting** the handcuffs on me, I would have never thought that my life was being saved in that very moment. I had never taken an X-ray for anything. So, for me to find out that my lungs were on the verge of collapsing and to being able to catch it in time is miraculous.

The proof that a higher power exist and that this power loves me and has a plan for me was evident. I said to myself, I'm giving off the correct energy. Authenticity is magnetic. I was unemployed and had no medical insurance. I had no way of paying for a six- figure surgery. With no symptoms or signs of fatigue, I would have been dead right now.

Going to jail literally saved my life on so many levels. There I was locked away as an enemy of the state, in a place that could either make me a better person or make me worse, and I came out smarter, stronger, healthier, and ready for the world. I would have never imagined that three years of incarceration would have made me the man I was intended to be. Three years I will never regret.

And yes, I still fight the demons of inadequacy at times, but I know my moment is coming. I just hate to hear the word "potential" at this point in my life. Potential is not secure. To exist only in possibility is not enough. I need to know I am. Status, purpose, I need to feel like a man. Potential in my opinion is for kids. At thirty-two, you either have it or you don't. We all search for that comfort and stability in our lives. Some achieve it sooner than others. Some give up without a fight, not understanding the sacrifices they needed to take. And some fight until death, only accomplishing the fight, and become content. From my journey, I realized that there's no format. There's no way or blueprint to do it. Too much over-thinking can result in nothing getting done at all. There's no way it's supposed to be done, just do it. The pieces will always fall in your favor. No matter how hard it is, if you truly feel in your heart, and I mean a feeling that is the center of your soul, then never give up. Never stop. Because trying and failing is easier to live with than not doing anything about it at all.

You don't ever want to look back at your life and wish you could have done more. Even though it feels like all those random occurrences in my life meant nothing at the time, it did. It was all part of a plan bigger than I could ever fathom. All you have in life is who you are and the passion that gives you the energy to pursue. Following who you are and what you want to do will lead you down bumpy roads. There will be detour signs leading you to a safer and stable destination. But remember, nothing worth having is easily attained. So, stay rooted in your orchard and never worry about what's growing across the field. Believe in your seed.

Even if you're the only one who sees it. When my wanting to be a rapper never happened, nothing broke more heart more. If it wasn't for my passion to be great, then I don't know where I'll be. There are life lessons you must learn in the pursuit of dreams that can only come from failure and disappointment. And if you're in it alone, then more than likely, in the pursuance of your dream, you will be knocked down and want to give up. Following your dreams will be hardest thing you'll ever do.

But the best decision you'll ever make will be believing in yourself against all odds. So, keep dreaming, even if it breaks your heart. And be patient, I don't mean wait. There's a saying floating around about waiting your turn. No. You don't wait your turn, you make your turn. Those who wait only get the scraps left behind by those who hustle. Being patience is more than waiting, it's the attitude you have while waiting. As time ticks by, the closer to being more than just a random thought away from living my dream seems feasible, when I look in the mirror, I'm reminded that I can do anything I plan to do. No matter what I accomplish today, in five years, I plan to be eons ahead as a business helping the youth find their passion. I'm still, no matter what I accomplish and how far I came, just a random thought away.

KEEP PUSHING